AF375477

MUNI
PRESS

Masaryk University Press
Brno / 2024

Mankind – Music – Technology

Technology in the Musical Thinking of the 20th and Early 21st Centuries

Translated by Mark Newkirk

Martin Flašar

Book reviewed by Prof. Leigh Landy, director of the Music, Technology and Innovation –
Institute for Sonic Creativity (MTI²), De Montfort University, Leicester
and Prof. MgA. Mgr. Michal Rataj, Ph.D., professor of the Music and Dance Faculty
of the Academy of Performing Arts in Prague.

On the cover: Detail of the interactive exhibition Garden of Fantasy and Music (EXPO 2005, Aichi). From the left: organ by Václav Smolka, pool with piano and caterpillar with a camera obscura by Petr Nikl, and Dripping Machine by Milan Cais. Source: Archive of Petr Nikl.

ISBN 978-80-280-0364-7
ISBN 978-80-280-0365-4 (online ; pdf)

https://doi.org/10.5817/CZ.MUNI.M280-0365-2024

Table of Contents

Acknowledgements

This book is the result of the author's long-term interest in the music of the 20th century and of the 21st century as it is now unfolding. It is also the result of his life-long interest in technology. In addition, the chapters that follow are the distillate of more than ten years of experience with leading training and lecture courses at the Masaryk University Department of Musicology devoted to music in the context of new media, electronic music, and aesthetic conceptions of multimedia. It has therefore passed the tests of time, of discussions with students and colleagues, and above all of repetition. Those tests wash facts of lesser importance away and bring inconsistency in argumentation to light.

First, I would like to take this opportunity to thank my inspirational teachers not only at the Department of Musicology of the Faculty of Arts, but also throughout Masaryk University because teachers shape not only students, but often also future teachers. At my age, I can also perhaps afford to thank my students who have inspired me with their papers or even just by their comments during lectures. I am very grateful to the Faculty of Arts of Masaryk University for providing financial support, thanks to which I have been able to spend a number of enriching days at the library of De Montfort University in Leicester, without which this study would have lacked the necessary framework of current discourse. I also wish to thank Prof. Leigh Landy, director of the Music, Technology and Innovation – Institute for Sonic Creativity (MTI^2) at De Montfort University in Leicester for supporting mutual collaboration.

Last but not least, I would like to thank my parents for providing me with a musical education in addition to free access to an Atari 800XE computer at the turn of the 1980s and '90s and later to a PC 286, with which most Czech households definitely were not routinely furnished in those days. And I owe a debt of special thanks to my wife, who temporarily put this study ahead of her own interests and unhesitatingly read it and made comments.

Martin Flašar, Brno, 2023

Chapter 1

Introduction

"As far as academia is concerned, technology is not discussed at all [...]. Apparently, this carries with it the conviction that technology concerns particular secondary aspects of life with which certain people must involve themselves, but that do not apply to mankind as such. The conflicts that technology is now causing in human societies, born paradoxically of those societies' own productivity, are beginning to bring to the attention of even those who are most blinded the unhealthy remoteness from the human destiny, i.e. from real life, in which academia has found itself."

José Ortega y Gasset: *Úvod: Universita a technika*[1]

The question of technology and of its function in human life, culture, and the arts is surely deserving of greater attention than has so far been devoted to it. Already in 1933, the Spanish philosopher José Ortega y Gasset wrote:

"Without technology, mankind would not exist and could never have existed. [...] There can be no doubt that technology has long since become one of the unavoidable conditions of human life in such a way that present-day mankind could not exist without it, even if it wished to do so. Today, mankind no longer lives in nature, but instead makes its home in supernature, which it has created in a new day of Genesis: in technology."[2]

The dependence of human existence upon technology also applies to human thought and creativity. Therefore, even music as a product of human thought is not possible without the use of technology. Music employs not only technological instruments, but also rational procedures for its production, organisation, distribution, and perception. Technology is more than just an artefact of Western

---

1   ORTEGA Y GASSET, José. *Úvaha o technice* [Meditación de la técnica y otros ensayos sobre ciencia y filosofía]. Praha: OIKOYMENH, 2011, p. 13. Note: the translator of this book has himself translated all quotes from referenced Czech-language materials unless otherwise indicated.

2   Ibid., p. 12.

culture. It is a model for thought and the formation of relationships, as we are reminded by Carlos Gustavo Guerra.[3] Others like Collins and Young go even farther, postulating that:

> "[...] music is a technology—the production and dissemination of music is a technological system, a system whose affordances have the ability to shape not only the musical content but also the extent to which music can be produced and distributed. On that basis, changes in technology are an integral part of the story of music."[4]

Aden Evens adds:

> "Sound, especially musical sound, does not generally arise spontaneously but is generated through certain techniques and by using certain technologies. The materiality of music weds it to technology, which enables its production and dissemination. The experience of music thus demands a technical understanding of musical technologies."[5]

One of the first texts I got my hands on as a beginning musicology student was *Úvod do hudební vědy* (An Introduction to Musicology) by Jiří Fukač and Ivan Poledňák.[6] In one of the early chapters on history, Fukač tried to use a reference to Boethius's treatise *De institutione musica* as an argument bolstering the historical relevance of musicology. In the treatise, Boethius divides the scope of the term "musica" as part of a holistic, hierarchically arranged theory of the universe into *musica mundana*, *musica humana*, and *musica instrumentalis*. Out of respect for authorities (of the early Middle Ages and of relatively contemporary times), we are taking the liberty of borrowing this concept and applying it to the present-day situation. With a clear conscience, it seems, we can abandon Boethius's model of *musicae mundanae* based on the period idea of the harmony of the spheres, but we will stop to consider the other two categories. The relationship between human music (*musica humana*) and instrumental music (*musica instrumentalis*) can be regarded as being at the core of our study. We shall attempt to point out the various modalities of relationships between mankind, music, and technology, which vary on a scale from utopian ideas about the influence of technology on musical thinking to sceptical approaches that can lead to a re-evaluation of technology's function. I think composers' and musicians' attitudes towards new technologies are key to understanding music of the 20th and newly beginning 21st centuries.

---

3   GUERRA, Carlos Gustavo. The Mechanization of Intelligence and the Human Aspects of Music. In Eduardo Reck Miranda (ed.). *Readings in Music and Artificial Intelligence*. Harwood academic publishers, 2000, p. 207.

4   COLLINS, Steve and YOUNG, Sherman. *Beyond 2.0: The Future of Music*. Equinox Publishing, 2014, p. 9.

5   EVENS, Aden. *Music, Machines and Experience: Theory out of Bounds*. Vol. 27. University of Minnesota Press, Minneapolis, 2005, Preface, p. xi.

6   FUKAČ, Jiří and POLEDŇÁK, Ivan. *Úvod do hudební vědy*. Univerzita Palackého v Olomouci, 2001, p. 65.

1.1 Subject matter and methodology of research

The basic question that this book raises is how the development of technology, its relation to music, and the development of mankind's attitudes towards technology in the process of musical production have transformed musical thinking in the realm of art music composed in the 20th and early 21st centuries.

A term that is central to this publication is musical thinking, which has defined the form taken by musicology not only in Brno, but throughout this country in the hands of Otakar Zich and especially Vladimír Helfert. The latter based an objective method of studying a musical work on the analysis of two fundamental elements: the source of inspiration and the musical structure. By "source of inspiration", Helfert means the conditions and stimuli from which an artwork arises, i.e., artists' personalities and the milieu in which the artists live, including the intellectual and aesthetic currents that influence them.[7]

> "[...] the focal point of interest of a critical history of the arts must be critical *knowledge of the artwork*. This mostly means knowing the static structure of the artwork, its internal laws, its melodic, harmonic, formal, or coloristic features, and its relationship to the words being set to music (where relevant). One must also know the dynamic context of these statically recognised values with the musical values that surrounded the work in the present and the past, i.e., one must know the context in music history, and on that dual basis must arrive at a synthetic picture of the individual (or eclectic) nature of the artwork [...]."[8]

The central point of interest of this book is then the transformation of musical thinking under the conditions of the new technologies and aesthetic currents that reflect their creation.

The relationship between mankind (society), music, and technology, which is developing in an Euro-American cultural and historical context, can be expressed by the following model (Fig. 1).

No single element in this model of interdependence can be eliminated. There is no music without mankind because music is fundamentally a human creation, and if we object to the contrary (e.g., birdsong or algorithmically generated compositions), mankind remains as the recipient who gives meaning to the set of sounds in question and understands it as a logical system. Music therefore need not necessarily be produced as music, but music must be perceived at least in the sensualistic sense of Berkeley's dictum *"esse est percipi"*, not to mention the rationalistic perspective according to which we might only imagine music that is not necessarily heard. In any case, music depends upon human cognitive processes.

---

7   HELFERT, Vladimír. *Česká moderní hudba. Studie o české hudební tvořivosti.* Olomouc: Index, 1936, pp. V–VII.

8   Ibid., p. VII.

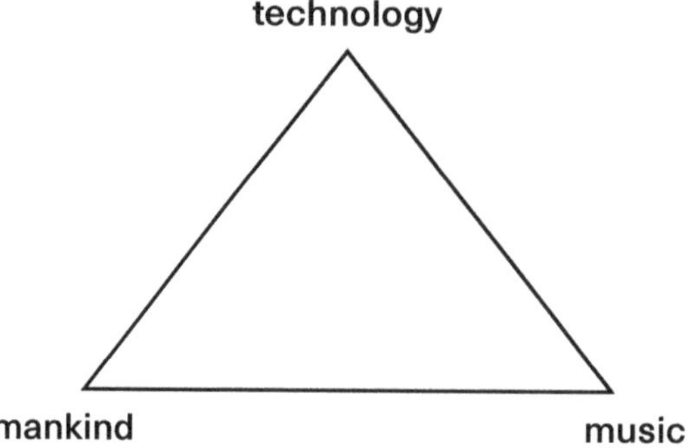

Fig. 1 Defining of the field of research in question.

Technology (or technique as its subset) is another necessary condition for the existence of music (compositional technique, singing technique, instrumental technique, the technical design of instruments, reproduction technology etc.). Nonetheless, artificially separating technology from the field of music enables us to analyse the question in a broader context (social, historical, and aesthetic).

The relationships to be examined in this study based on the triadic model shown above are:

1. Development of technology (instruments, instrumentation) in relation to art music.
2. Transformation of music (as an artefact or process) under the influence of new technologies.
3. Musical thinking in art music of the 20th and early 21st centuries as a consequence of technological transformations.

These three basic elements are also reflected in the communication model of music, which is an adaption of the Shannon-Weaver linear transmission model of communication:[9]

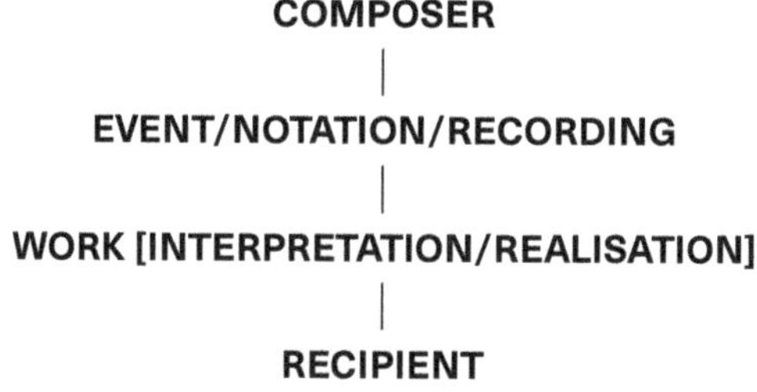

This is a model of a one-way flow of musical information from the composer to the recipient (or even beyond for reflections and meta-reflection on music). For our

9   Cf. FUKAČ, Jiří. *Pojmosloví hudební komunikace*. Brno: Masarykova univerzita, 1991, p. 53.

purposes, we will be dealing with the first half of the model between the composer and the work, i.e., the production of music. Note that the section of the model called "event/notation/recording" refers to ways that a musical work is created or comes into being. The music arises either as a live event (improvisation), a fixed structure of ideas in musical notation, or the creation of a work directly in an audio medium (e.g., *musique concrète*, electroacoustic music).

This book will not be dealing with the transformation of the reception and consumption of music through technology (nor with the questions of reception habits, environments, music distribution etc.) because that area of research requires an entirely different methodology.

After the introductory chapters of definitions, contextualisation, theoretical issues, and aesthetics more generally, this volume presents several case studies on individual creative poetics that have something to tell us about the changing attitudes of creative musicians (performers and composers) towards technologies during the 20th and 21st centuries.

It is our belief that the goal of musicology as an arts-related discipline of the humanities should not be just to ask questions of agency like "how?" (as, for example, in the case of music theory), but also to ask ontological questions like "why?". This rule also applies to the relationship between music and technology. It is clear that heretofore, questions of the relationship between technology and music have been limited almost exclusively to asking "how?" instead of "why?" and to the examination of context.[10] We lack knowledge of the causes and interpretations of why the music of the 20th century, which definitely is a domain of technology (both analogue and digital), happens to exist in the form that is familiar to us. Being more than just one of many factors in music, technology is really the key to understanding the music of the 20th century. Technology cannot be avoided in music of the 20th century; regarding it, one can only take one of the stances stated below. So far, the existing literature has devoted itself relatively one-sidedly to the perspective of technology used for the (re)production of music, and not to the perspective of the music itself, which is transformed by that technology.

In view of the historical nature of the question at hand of the problem of the relationship between music, technology, and mankind, which spans the 20th and early 21st centuries, one must take into consideration theories now regarded as outdated in many ways, such as technological determinism. In this critical reflection on technology, one can demarcate more narrowly the relationship between music and technology in musical thinking. The modalities of coexistence of the two areas can be expressed by movement along a scale depending upon the intensity of mutual interaction (dominance of one of the areas) from a strongly positive to a somewhat positive, a somewhat negative, and finally a strongly negative (critical) attitude.

---

10   For notable exceptions, cf. LANDY, Leigh. *Understanding the Art of Sound Organization*. Cambridge, Mass.: MIT Press, c2007, p. 36ff; EMMERSON, Simon and LANDY, Leigh (eds.). *Expanding the Horizon of Electroacoustic Music Analysis*. Cambridge: Cambridge University Press, 2016, p. 11ff.

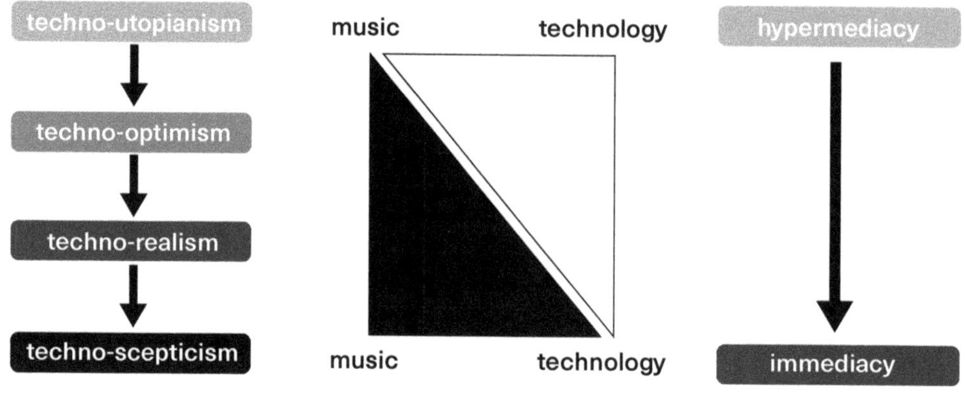

Fig. 2 The range of people's attitudes towards technology in music with respect to the function of technology in music.

Techno-utopianism (technological utopianism, largely synonymous with technological determinism). Music is in a submissive position with respect to technology, to which absolute value is assigned in this case. It is assumed automatically that technological innovations will lead to a (positive) change of musical thinking and expression. From the perspective of Bolter's and Grusin's theory of remediation,[11] one finds here the application of the logic of hypermediation, i.e., the tendency to make a particular technology visible. (We find these tendencies for example in Feruccio Busoni's *Entwurf einer neuen Ästhetik der Tonkunst*, in Luigi Russolo's manifesto *L'Arte dei rumori*, and in John Cage's book *The Future of Music: Credo*.)

Difficult to differentiate from techno-utopianism, **techno-optimism** (technological optimism, technicism) is an attitude that perceives technology as a source of inspiration or as determinative (e.g., Honegger: *Pacific 231*; Reich: *Different Trains*; dodecaphony, serialism, stochastic music etc.).

Techno-realism (technological realism). The relationship and function of music and technology are balanced. This is an instrumental relationship; here, technology is given the role of agency for music. Composers assign technology a strictly defined instrumental function in relation to the musical work. The work and its idea are primary (e.g. Stravinsky and his poetics; Varèse: *Déserts*; Boulez: *Répons*; Saariaho and her creative aesthetic).

Techno-scepticism (technological scepticism, technological pessimism, techno-dystopianism). Music rejecting technology as an end in itself or as determinative.

A **post-technological** attitude has a sense of the overcoming of the conditionality of music by electronic technology and belief in its potential for innovation. With

---

11   BOLTER, Jay David and GRUSIN, Richard Arthur. *Remediation: Understanding New Media*. Cambridge, Mass.: MIT Press, 2000.

respect to remediation theory, one can use the term immediation, which designates a tendency to disguise the use of technology for the sake of presentation of the work (e.g. Ligeti: *Atmosphères*, the creative aesthetics of N. Collins or J. Richards).

This range of attitudes towards technology overlaps partially with David Chandler's typology,[12] where within the framework of criticism of technological determinism, the author differentiates between:

— **hard technological determinism** – technology as an exclusive factor of changes to social behaviour;
— **soft technological determinism** – technology as a key factor in changes, but not the only one;
— **sociocultural determinism** – technology shaped by the societal and cultural context; and
— **voluntarism** – technology fully controlled by the subject's intentional approach.

In our case, we are not examining the impact of technology on social behaviour, but instead its influence on individual musical thinking and creativity. From the degree of dependence or value of technology in the creative process, we derive the individual categories of attitudes of creative artists to technology. These categories will be explored in more detail in individual chapters.

1.2 Definitions of basic terms

We can use a whole range of approaches to define the basic terms used in this study. From the set of types of definitions offered in *Úvod do ontologie*[13] (Introduction to Ontology) by Josef Šmajs and Josef Krob, we have chosen the following for use in this book:

1. enumeration of all **elements** belonging to the defined class,
2. enumeration of **properties** of objects of the given class, i.e., descriptive definition,
3. **contextual definition**, which defines by using the term being explained in a context from which the meaning of the term in question is implied by the overall meaning. For our study, this type of definition seems to be the most natural. It enables the defining of a technology in the context of its function connected with the production of art music of the 20th and early 21st centuries.

---

12   CHANDLER, Daniel. Shaping and Being Shaped: Engaging With Media. *Computer-Mediated Communication Magazine* [online]. 1996. [Accessed on 13 Sept. 2010]. Retrieved from: http://www.aber.ac.uk/media/Documents/short/determ.html.

13   ŠMAJS, Josef and KROB, Josef. *Úvod do ontologie* [online]. [Accessed on 15 July 2017]. Retrieved from: https://www.phil.muni.cz/fil/eo/skripta/kapitola_1.html. 2nd edition corrected and expanded. Brno: Masarykova univerzita Brno, 1994. (1st edition 1991).

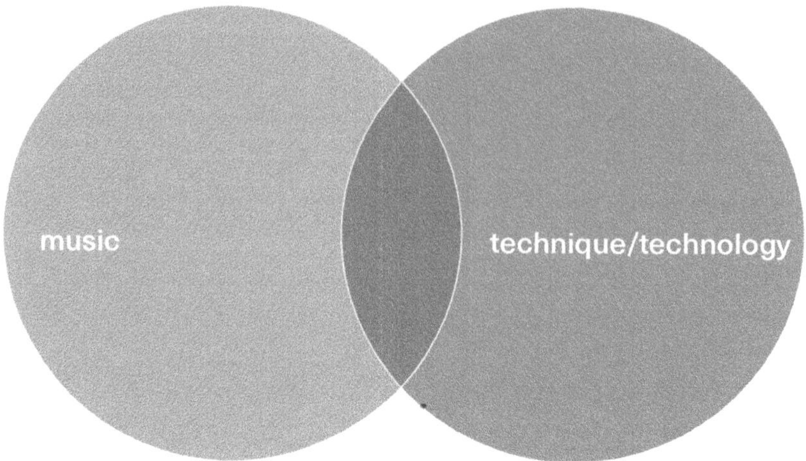

Fig. 3 Intersection of the semantic fields of the terms "music" and "technique/technology".

Since "technology" is a transversal term that comes from a wide variety of spheres of human thought and action, its contextualised definition must be sought in fields and disciplines that are closely interconnected with music, such as aesthetics and sociology.

In *Encyklopedie estetiky*[14] (Encyclopaedia of Aesthetics), the economy of the efforts at defining words is surprising, and the entry for the Czech word "technika" (technology, technique) is one of the briefest. I think the following passage is the most helpful:

"'Technika' [technique, technology] is a conscious and directed approach capable of being reproduced and transferred. It is a way of doing things in any area, and not just in industrial manufacturing or the applied sciences: there can be techniques of craftsmanship and techniques of an empirical or even irrational character (e.g. techniques based on the use of magical knowledge). The practical value of individual techniques rests in the effectiveness with which they are capable of achieving the desired result."[15]

While there is an allowance for the possibility of technology of an irrational nature, the interpretation is clearly erroneous. Although one can imagine magical rituals based on an irrational belief, their performance and application are always rational acts because they are working with the assumption of logical causality (an action followed by a reaction). The author determines the value of a technology from its potential to enable achieving the intended result. In other words, this is a teleological definition of technology.[16]

---

14   SOURIAU, Anne. Technika [entry]. In SOURIAU, Étienne. *Encyklopedie estetiky*. Praha: Victoria Publishing, 1994, p. 858.

15   Ibid.

16   Also cf. TONDL, Ladislav. *Věda, technika a společnost: Soudobé tendence a transformace vzájemných vazeb.* Praha: FILOSOFIA, 1994, p. 106.

On the other hand, the entry for "technika" in the *Velký sociologický slovník*[17] (Large Dictionary of Sociology) presents a much lengthier exercise in lexicography. It explains that:

> "technika [...] [represents] all the artificially created procedures and products that are involved in human activities and social processes [...]. Today, technical products and procedures are so entangled with people's actions and have so much influence on diverse forms of coexistence and on the conditions of life that the question of the nature of technology arises with respect to the consequences of their functioning in society and their subordination to human purposes."[18]

It is the area of the collision between technology and human purposes that represents the subject of our investigation. On a general level, this involves the dynamic delineation of the degree of mutual interaction and influence of the sphere of technology and the sphere of human thinking and creativity. However, the problem is more complicated than the dictionary entry would admit. The dichotomy between the world of technology and the human world is a mere theoretical illusion because technology is just the extension and application of human thought and action, and not an isolated entity.

The text of the entry also mentions two categories of "technika" in a narrower and a broader sense respectively. The narrower sense refers to material resources for action towards a purpose, meaning machines, tools, instruments etc., as well as transformational procedures. The broader sense refers to *procedures of action and thought, which abide by methodical rules of operation and lead to a definite strategic goal.*[19] It must be emphasised that in this definition, "technika" becomes the common strategy for all human activity including the arts and sciences. That fact also becomes one of the initial premises of this book, which understands science, the arts, and technology as areas of realisation of human thinking, which become interrelated to varying degrees.

Then in the entry for the Czech word *"technologie"*, the same dictionary warns us that in the Czech language, the terms "technika" and "technologie" overlap, so those Czech words are understood in this study as synonyms.[20] We may furthermore regard technology or technique as a set of applications of results of research in the natural or applied sciences. The problem of the relationship between technique (or technology) and music at the highest level is a question of the relationship between music and the natural sciences.

As we continue with basic definitions by the method of focusing, i.e., gradually drawing nearer to the area being examined at the cost of narrowing our field of view,

---

17   MüK. Technika [entry]. In *Velký sociologický slovník*. II, P-Ž. Praha: Karolinum, 1996, pp. 1278–1279.
18   Ibid., p. 1278.
19   Ibid., p. 1279.
20   Ibid., p. 1283.

we arrive at the definition of "technika" in *Slovník české hudební kultury*[21] (Dictionary of Czech Musical Culture). There, the problem is divided into several parts in which "technika" is defined in various contexts. The entry, written by Jiří Fukač and Jana Pavlíčková, defines "technika" as a set of procedures and resources (especially instruments) that serve to supply what is needed in connection with music.[22] Since the 19th century, the term "technika" has been used in relation to music with other meanings:

1. Technique of playing, singing, or interpreting in general (etudes, instrumental method books).
2. Compositional technique (counterpoint, orchestration, the rationalistic procedures of 20th-century music).
3. Technique of making musical instruments.
4. Reproduction technology (in certain cases, the difference between production and reproduction is not obvious, such as in *musique concrète*).
5. Technology as the subject matter, inspiration for, and formative factor of a musical work.

From amongst these explanations of the word "technika", in this book we will be using numbers 2 through 5. The technique of making instruments usually precedes the concept of a musical composition, which is written in most cases for a particular instrument that restricts the range of the composer's ideas. Technology thus does not directly predetermine the result of the creative process, but it provides the conditions for the change of social and cultural practices.[23] It is also for this reason that in the musical poetics of the 20th century (F. Busoni, L. Russolo, J. Cage, E. Varèse, K. Stockhausen et al.) we often find discussion of the need for new instruments that will enable the creation of new music. Electronic reproduction technology is put at the level of instruments just to enable us to consider whether musical instruments are not just a special kind of reproduction technology.

1.3 Framework of discourse and the present state of research

The basic frame of discourse for what follows consists of systematic musicology and especially musical aesthetics as a specialised philosophy of the arts, along with music theory and musical sociology. A diachronic aspect is represented by the chronological arrangement of the material of certain chapters.

Hierarchically, the highest disciplines in which the chosen approaches intersect are philosophy and musicology. The tradition of philosophical thinking provides us

---

21 FUKAČ, Jiří and PAVLÍČKOVÁ, Jana. Technika [entry]. In VYSLOUŽIL, Jiří and FUKAČ, Jiří. *Slovník české hudební kultury*. Praha: Editio Supraphon, 1997, pp. 920–921.

22 Ibid., p. 920.

23 COLLINS and YOUNG, op. cit., p. 11.

with the conditions for intellectual reflection on technology involving consideration of the essence of this question in relation to mankind and society, or, for example, reflection on the ontological status of a technological work, while musicology offers an analytical, interpretive, and pragmatic framework of interpretation. Concerning the philosophy of technology, there are two treatises we should mention as being of primary importance for the purposes of this book: *Die Frage nach Technik* (The Question Concerning Technology) by Martin Heidegger and *Meditación de la técnica* (Meditation on Technics) by José Ortega y Gasset.[24]

Because a number of incorrect assumptions and rigid categories in the realm of theory have persisted to the present, hindering our view of the music of the 20th and 21st centuries, we would like to devote this study (with an awareness of the difficulty of such an intention) to expanding our ideas about newer and contemporary music and to offer new perspectives on relations between music and technology in the music of the last century and of the present one.

There is not a large quantity of foreign literature, let alone Czech literature, dealing with the relationship between music and technology at a general level. It is remarkable how successfully this area of inquiry escapes theoretical reflection. If we find a publication with "music and technology" or some variation thereof in its title, upon opening the publication we find that it amounts to a practical handbook for musicians or sound designers on how to use specific technologies to achieve a particular result, or else the publication is devoted to the influence of technology on the distribution and reception of music.

We find meagre numbers of foreign publications focusing on the relationship between music and technology, and in what we do find, we discover that their topics are so disparate and narrowly specialised that they are of little help with creating a consistent view of the issue. For example, there are the proceedings of the event *Music and Technology*[25] held by UNESCO in Stockholm in 1970. Other collective monographs in this field are of a similarly fragmented character, e.g. *Music and Technologies* (2013)[26] and *Music and Technologies 2* (2014),[27] where studies on computer music are found alongside discussions of architecture. Reference works like the *Oxford Handbooks* series can also be rather problematical. They mostly cover narrowly specialised topics, but they do not other a synthesised view of the topic of "music and technology". Next page brings a selective list of the existing handbooks that have at least something to say about the relationship between music and technology.

---

24   HEIDEGGER, Martin. *The Question Concerning Technology and Other Essays*. Translated and with an introduction by William Lovitt. New York & London: Garland Publishing Inc., 1977; ORTEGA Y GASSET, José, op. cit.

25   Paris: La Revue musicale, 1971.

26   KUČINSKAS, Darius and DAVISMOON, Stephen. *Music and Technologies*. Newcastle upon Tyne: Cambridge Scholars Publishing, 2013.

27   KUČINSKAS, Darius and KENNAWAY, George. *Music and Technologies 2*. Newcastle upon Tyne: Cambridge Scholars Publishing, 2014.

- PINCH, Trevor and BIJSTERVELD, Karin (eds.). *The Oxford Handbook of Sound Studies*. Oxford: Oxford University Press, 2012.
- RICHARDSON, John, Claudia GORBMAN and Carol VERNALLIS (eds.). *The Oxford Handbook of New Audiovisual Aesthetics*. Oxford: Oxford University Press, 2013.
- DEAN, Roger T. (ed.). *The Oxford Handbook of Computer Music*. New York: Oxford University, 2009.
- VERNALLIS, Carol, HERZOG, Amy and RICHARDSON, John (eds.). *The Oxford Handbook of Sound and Image in Digital Media*. Oxford: Oxford University Press, 2013.
- NEUMEYER, David (ed.). *The Oxford Handbook of Film Music Studies*. Oxford: Oxford University Press, c2014.
- COLLINS, Karen, KAPRALOS, Bill and TESSLER, Holly (eds.). *The Oxford Handbook of Interactive Audio*. Oxford: Oxford University Press, 2014.
- GOPINATH, Sumanth and STANYEK, Jason (eds.). *The Oxford Handbook of Mobile Music Studies, Volume 1*. Oxford: Oxford University Press, 2014.
- GOPINATH, Sumanth and STANYEK, Jason (eds.). *The Oxford Handbook of Mobile Music Studies, Volume 2*. Oxford: Oxford University Press, 2014.
- WHITELEY, Sheila and RAMBARRAN, Shara (eds.). *The Oxford Handbook of Music and Virtuality*. Oxford: Oxford University Press, 2016.

The subfield of musicology that seems to be the closest to the question we are investigating is *technomusicology*. Upon closer inspection we find that this really is just an academic course taught by Wayne Marshall at Harvard University. The course contents are the history of the reproduction of sound, technical mediation of sound, soundscapes, radio, podcasting, sampling, the aesthetics of mashup, video montage (YouTube), sound mixing for DJs, videogame design, working with music, and interactivity.[28] Although the course draws on academic literature, its clear focus is on practice and the practical utility of its methods. Even just a cursory glance at Marshall's publication profile clearly shows that his departure point is mainly the milieu of Afro-American popular culture and that he is developing a fruitful discourse with broadly conceived Anglo-American ethnomusicology. It is just a pity that the author has not published a text with a systematic overview dealing with his conception of technomusicology.

Another interesting representative of technologically oriented musicology is Kiri Miller from Brown University (USA). Her departure point is also ethnomusicology, and her research focuses on digital games, popular culture, and gender studies. Her most recent major publication is the book *Playable Bodies: Dance Games and Intimate Media* (New York: Oxford University Press, 2017). At Brown University she offers such courses as the ethnomusicology seminar *Music and Technoculture*. The course contents are ethnographic approaches to technologically mediated musical practices. The focus is on the recording studio, electronic dance music, mass media, digital gaming, virtual reality, multimedia installations, and the reception of popular music. The

---

28   *Music 190r: Technomusicology* [online]. [Accessed on 5 Sept. 2016]. Retrieved from: http://wayneand-wax.com/academic/Music190r-syllabus.pdf.

newly emerging field of ludomusicology is also represented by such scholars Karen Collins and Melanie Fritsch.

In both cases, the focus is on a broader musical culture and often on heteronomously functional music with the use of an ethnographic approach that studies music as the outcome of the actions of specific individuals and of their groups, and that deals with the question of various audiences.

Social theory constitutes an important sphere of discourse within the given framework. Collins and Young[29] confront several theories of the relationship between mankind (society) and technology. The first, technological determinism, takes as its departure point the theory of Marshall McLuhan, who understands mechanical technology as an extension of our limbs and electronic technology as an extension of our nervous system.[30] He attributes to technology a decisive share in our perceptions and thinking.

Another approach that is becoming an alternative to rigid technological determinism can be called "conditioning".[31] Paul Levinson later discusses "soft" and "hard" determinism (analogous to conditioning and determinism respectively).[32]

Wiebe Bijker's technological constructivism (*Social Construction of Technology; SCOT*)[33] approaches the problem from the opposite direction. This is a theory created as an antipole to technological determinism, which treats technology and human action as a single, dynamic whole. In the theory, various social groups attribute different meanings to various technologies. The identity of technologies is therefore societally consensual and flexible.

The proposed solution for the relationship between mankind and technology with perhaps the most compromises is Bruno Latour's *actor-network theory (ANT)*.[34] (The author jokes that there are "four things that do not work with actor-network theory; the word actor, the word network, the word theory and the hyphen!") This theory is also promoted by Madeleine Akrich, Michael Callon, and John Law. It understands all systems as a network of *actants*, encompassing not only human, but also non-human factors (i.e. both subjects and technological objects). The ability to act is thus also attributed to inanimate entities. From this perspective we can, for example,

---

29   COLLINS, Steve and YOUNG, Sherman. *Beyond 2.0: The Future of Music*. Equinox Publishing, 2014.

30   Ibid., p. 12.

31   WINNER, Langdon. *Autonomous Technology: Technics out of Control as a Theme in Political Thought*. Cambridge, MA: MIT Press, 1977, pp. 192–210.

32   LEVINSTON, Paul. *The Soft Edge: A Natural History and Future of the Information Revolution*. London: Routledge 1997, p. 3.

33   PINCH, Trevor and BIJKER, Wiebe. The Social Construction of Facts and Artifacts: Or How the Sociology of Science and the Sociology of Technology Might Benefit Each Other. In Wiebe Bijker, Thomas Hughes and Trevor Pinch (eds). *The Social Construction of Technological Systems: New Directions in the Sociology and History of Technology*. Cambridge, MA: MIT Press, 2012, pp. 17–50.

34   Cf. CALLON, Michael and LATOUR, Bruno. Unscrewing the Big Leviathan: How Actors Macro-Structure Reality and How Sociologists Help Them to Do So. In Karin Knorr-Cetina and Aron V. Cicourel (eds). *Advances in Social Theory and Methodology: Towards an Integration of Micro and Macro-Sociology*. Boston: Routledge, 2014, pp. 277–303.

understand the system of culture as the result of not only people's mutual interaction, but also the interactions between people and technologies, people and animals etc. *"According to Latour, technological artefacts can be described as anthropomorphic in three senses: they have been made by people, they substitute for human action (human acts are delegated to them; they substitute for human actors), and they shape human behaviour."*[35] An important component of this theory is the act of *translation*, whereby the ideas of engineers define the form of technological artefacts, which in turn influence their users (so the user becomes the object of the artefact).[36] This dynamic, non-hierarchical system probably best corresponds to the focus of our study, but one probably cannot simply assent to the categorisation of this theory as post-humanistic thinking, precisely because of the fact that technology is perceived as anthropomorphic.

In one of the most penetrating publications on our topic, Timothy D. Taylor's *Strange Sounds: Music, Technology and Culture*[37] classifies socio-technological theories as follows:

1. Voluntaristic approach – technology is a neutral tool that people use. It becomes good or bad based on how it is used.
2. Technological determinism – the assertion that technology directly transforms its user.
3. Technological somnambulism (Langdon Winner) – this refers to a non-critical approach to technology. Whatever a technology's characteristics may be, it is the product of technical thinking, and as a mere tool it is undeserving of special interest or reflection.

Our point of departure is closest to a voluntaristic approach, but the possibilities and arguments of technological determinism must also be examined. We think the third category is too remote from reality as considered rationally.

Menser and Aronowitz[38] define three basic methodologies for investigating the position of technology in society not only as an artefact, but also as a part of practice:

1. ontological – determines what technology is and focuses on the object;
2. pragmatic – takes an interest in on how technology is used and what skills and knowledge are based on its use (DJing, computer hacking etc.);

---

35   MAREŠ, Jakub. „*Ne-sociologie*": *pojetí modernosti Bruno Latoura*. Diploma thesis. Supervisor: doc. PhDr. Jiří Šubrt, CSc. FF UK v Praze, 2009., p. 40.

36   LATOUR, Bruno. The Trouble with Actor-Network Theory [online]. [Accessed on 8 Oct. 2015]. *Philosophia* 1997, 25. Retrieved from: http://www.ensmp.fr/~latour/popart/p67.html.

37   TAYLOR, Timothy D. *Strange Sounds: Music, Technology and Culture*. NY, London: Routledge, 2001, p. 26.

38   ARONOWITZ, S., MARTINSONS, B. and MENSER, M. (eds.). On Cultural Studies. In *Technoscience and Cyber Culture*. NY: Routledge, 1996, p. 15, quoted in Lysloff, René T. A. – Gay, Leslie C. (eds.). *Music and Technoculture*. Middleton: Wesleyan University Press, 2003.

3. phenomenological – studies the impact of technology on human experience in the sense of indirect ties to its original function and aims to go beyond the limits of routine usage, e.g. a car symbolises youth, fashion, masculinity etc.

For our further discourse, we will largely be keeping to the first two approaches, which we understand as the key functions of technology in the music of the 20th and 21st centuries. On the basis of the aforementioned methodologies, Menser and Aronowitz describe three kinds of human, culturally determined behaviour closely connected with technologies:

1. interaction – direct handling of technology (driving a car, playing a piano etc.);
2. knowledge – understanding the importance of equipment or of a phenomenon; we learn what it can or is supposed to do (from an intuitive grasp to detailed scientific understanding);
3. experience – demands understanding of technology of the past and present (future). Considering technology in relation to various aspects of life (e.g. understanding the piano in all social contexts: belonging to a social class, level of education etc.). And because technologies can offer various possibilities of meaning, they often generate new desires, needs, and manners of use.

Like Latour, these two authors arrive at a model of a dynamic, closed system in which technologies are acculturated in societies primarily through human behaviour or usage, and at the same time they generate new needs and social spaces for mankind.[39] It is the ontological and especially the pragmatic functions of technology in contemporary music that constitute the two fundamental perspectives for investigation employed in this study.

Another evident, very strong tendency in academic circles abroad is a departure from the study of pure music as an isolated medium, instead moving towards transmedia overlaps and **multimedia** complexes. This tendency has its own developmental logic: it has been the media and technologies of the 20th century (film, radio, television, computers, internet etc.) that have brought the phenomena of the crossing of media boundaries (transmediality), the overlapping of media (intermediality), and the merging of media (multimediality) into creative practice. We already find attempts to reflect upon these tendencies in the manifesto *Futuristic Cinematography* (1916), in which F. T. Marinetti joins with others in calling film a synthetic, simultaneous, and poly-expressive symphony. There is a clear reference here to music as being developmentally the medium that is the most proximate and most comprehensive, which has been able to cope with the organisational elements of space-time and can become a model for multimedia. We find further extensions of reflection on music oriented towards multimedia in French-speaking (Michel Chion,

---

39   *"Technologies become imbedded in cultural systems and social institutions, which, in turn, are reconfigured by those same technologies"*, ibid., p. 8.

Jean-Yves Bosseur), German– (Dieter Daniels) and English-speaking milieus (Claudia Gorbman, Jamie Sexton, Randall Packer, and Ken Jordan). While Michel Chion[40] takes the traditions of Pierre Schaeffer's Groupe de Recherches Musicales (GRM) as his starting point and extends the principles of structural analysis of electronic music to film, Jean-Yves Bosseur's position[41] is intermedial: in a European context, he seeks out artistic statements at the boundaries of media and artistic genres centred in the Fluxus movement. In German circles, the work of Dieter Daniels[42] has been especially valuable, focusing on the media arts and the problem of audiovisuality in the arts. He summarised the outcome of this work in several collective monographs including *Audiovisuology* (2010–2015). From the English-speaking milieu, one must mention at least Claudia Gorbman[43] and her research on the function of sound and music in film, Jamie Sexton[44] and his work focusing on the multimedia context of sound and music, and especially the influential publication by Ken Jordan and Randall Packer[45] focused on a historically and technologically broad conception of multimedia.

In our Czech-speaking milieu, the question of the relationship between music and technology in the post-war period was first addressed in the field of "cybernetic" or **electroacoustic music**. In general, the bulk of discourse from the 1950s until the 1990s can be said to have been limited to electroacoustic music (or "EA music"). After the pioneering publications of Vladimír Lébl[46] and Eduard Herzog,[47] who were members of the Cybernetics Committee of the Union of Czechoslovak Composers, this mainly involves the work of Miroslav Kaduch.[48] In the new political and

---

40   His key treatise *Audio-vision: Sound on Screen* (Translation by Claudia Gorbman, Columbia University Press, 1994) was followed by several others devoted mainly to the relationship between the image and sound in film.

41   *Le sonore et le visuel – Intersections musique-arts plastiques aujourd'hui* (Les presses du réel, 1992).

42   FRIELING, Rudolf and DANIELS, Dieter (eds.). *Medien Kunst Netz 1 / Media Art Net 1: Medienkunst Im Uberblick / Survey of Media Art*. Birkhauser, 2004; DANIELS, Dieter, NAUMANN, Sandra and THOBEN, Jan (eds.). *See This Sound: Audiovisuology Compendium. An Interdisciplinary Survey of Audiovisual Culture*. Verlag der Buchhandlung Walther König, 2010; DANIELS, Dieter, NAUMANN, Sandra and THOBEN, Jan (eds.). *See This Sound: Audiovisuology 2. Essays*. Verlag der Buchhandlung Walther König, 2011. New edition: DANIELS, Dieter, NAUMANN, Sandra and THOBEN, Jan (eds.). *See This Sound: Audiovisuology Reader*. Verlag der Buchhandlung Walther König, 2015.

43   GORBMAN, Claudia. *Unheard Melodies: Narrative Film Music*. Indiana University Press, 1987.

44   SEXTON, Jamie (ed.). *Music, Sound and Multimedia: From the Live to the Virtual*. Edinburgh University Press, 2007.

45   PACKER, Randall and JORDAN, Ken. *Multimedia: From Wagner to Virtual Reality*. W. W. Norton & Company, 2002.

46   LÉBL, Vladimír and MOKRÝ, Ladislav. *Nové cesty hudby: sborník studií o novodobých skladebných směrech a vědeckých názorech na hudbu*. Praha: Státní hudební vydavatelství, 1964; LÉBL, Vladimír. *Elektronická hudba*. Praha: Státní hudební vydavatelství, 1966.

47   HERZOG, Eduard. *Nové cesty hudby: sborník studií o novodobých skladebných směrech a vědeckých pohledech na hudbu*. Praha: Editio Supraphon, 1970.

48   KADUCH, Miroslav. *Záznamová technika hudby XX. století*. Ostrava: Městské kulturní středisko v Ostravě, 1982.; KADUCH, Miroslav. *Česká a slovenská elektroakustická hudba 1964–1994: skladatelé, programátoři, technici, muzikologové, hudební kritici, publicisté: osobní slovník*. Ostrava: Miroslav Kaduch,

societal circumstances of the 1990s, the series of publications by Daniel Forró[49] in the edition Musitronika issued by the publisher Grada was outstanding for its comprehensiveness. Probably the most complete survey of the development of Czech EA music was compiled by Lenka Dohnalová,[50] although we do not find in it, for example, the development of EA music in Czech television and film, which is one of the key chapters of its development. Michal Rataj devoted himself more to radio art than to EA music in his book.[51] This is understandable given his employment at the radio station Český rozhlas 3 (for many years he was the author of the programme Radioateliér and the curator of the web portal Radiocustica). Rataj was the editor of the important collective monograph *Zvukem do hlavy* (With Sound into the Head),[52] which is devoted to the phenomenon of the acoustic arts in their various forms. The two-volume publication *Elektrofony* by Milan Guštar[53] is a major organological or organographic project of the relatively recent past. Another survey is the electronic publication *Elektroakustická hudba*[54] (Electroacoustic Music) by the author of this text.

The study *Technika a sociální funkčnost hudby*[55] (Technology and the Social Functionality of Music) by Jiří Fukač is an initial source of inspiration for us. It draws attention to the fact that discussion of the music–technology relationship encompasses so many different and contradictory approaches that one can hardly say anything consistent and homogenous about it. The following quote shows that there had hardly been any major progress in this area of research since the beginning of the 1970s: *"The new literature, which is solid and directly deals with the topic, is incapable of dealing with this ambiguity, and moreover (as usual), it is not written in the Czech language."*[56] Fukač recommends the expansion of consideration of the relationship of music and technology to include the presence of mankind and its activities. Fukač analyses the entire problem from three perspectives: 1: that of technology in the structure of music and its social consequences, 2: that of music in the structure of

---

1994.; KADUCH, Miroslav. *Vývojové aspekty české a slovenské elektroakustické hudby*. Ostrava: Miroslav Kaduch, 1997.

49 FORRÓ, Daniel. *MIDI: komunikace v hudbě*. V Praze: Grada, 1993. Musitronika; FORRÓ, Daniel. *Počítače a hudba*. Praha: Grada, 1994; FORRÓ, Daniel. *Domácí nahrávací studio*. Praha: Grada, 1996. Musitronika; FORRÓ, Daniel. *Svět MIDI*. Praha: Grada, 1997. Musitronika.

50 DOHNALOVÁ, Lenka. *Estetické modely evropské elektroakustické hudby a elektro-akustická hudba v ČR*. Praha: Univerzita Karlova, 2001.

51 RATAJ, Michal. *Elektroakustická hudba a vybrané koncepty radioartu: problematika vymezování tvůrčích pozic v prostředí akustických umění z pohledu domácí scény radioartu*. V Praze: Kant – Karel Kerlický pro AMU, 2007. Disk, Vol. 3.

52 RATAJ, Michal. *Zvukem do hlavy: sondy do současné audiokultury*. Praha: Akademie múzických umění v Praze, 2012.

53 GUŠTAR, Milan. *Elektrofony: historie, principy, souvislosti*. Část I, Elektromechanické nástroje. Praha: Uvnitř, 2007 a Část II, Elektronické nástroje. Praha: Uvnitř, 2008.

54 FLAŠAR, Martin. *Elektroakustická hudba* [online]. 1st edition. Brno: Masarykova univerzita, 2015. [Accessed on 18 Aug. 2016]. Elportál. Retrieved from: http://is.muni.cz/elportal/?id=1308636.

55 FUKAČ, Jiří. Technika a sociální funkčnost hudby. *Opus musicum*, 1972, No. 2, pp. 33–39.

56 Ibid., p. 33.

technology, and 3: the autonomous interaction of music and technology. In the first part, he mainly discusses the projection of the construction of musical instruments onto musical structure and compositional "technique". He also follows how technology can function as a motivating factor for changing group attitudes towards music (changes to practices in the consumption of music) or the creation of new groups of producers of technically innovative music (historical examples: instrumental music, operatic music, electronic music etc.). In the second part, he deals with the existence of music in the structure of technology, meaning how technology (in the present-day sense of mass media) takes part in the distribution, reception, consumption, and institutionalisation of interest groups or taste groups of listeners. The third part, perhaps the most interesting, discusses the potential existence of an area of overlap between music and technology (a kind of "musico-technology").[57] However speculative this proposal might seem, it might best correspond to reality, especially from the perspective of our present reading. While in 1972 Fukač wrote that musical-technological practices did not yet create a continuum but were too important a phenomenon with developmental potential for us to be able to ignore them, and today we can only confirm this thesis and regard it as the departure point for our work. Music truly cannot be separated from technology either at the level of thought and subsequent musical structure or at the level of interpretive and distributional practices or mere consumption, which is of a highly (inter)active character.

The symposium *Průmysl a technika v novodobé české kultuře* (Industry and Technology in Czech Culture of the Modern Era), held by the Institute of Art Theory and History of the Czech Academy of Sciences in Prague in 1985, was an interesting academic project that brought together various perspectives.[58] If we overlook the texts' mandatory Marxist rhetoric and ideology, this was probably the most synthesising attempt at serious debate on the topic in this country. There were only two contributions representing music at the symposium, and it makes sense to mention Ivan Vojtěch's text *Technika a hudební senzibilita* (Technology and Musical Sensibility). The author penetratingly points out that the technology of industrial society of the 19th century was already immediately being reflected in musical thinking and in theoretical reflections. Beginning with Hanslick[59] and Helmholtz,[60] music is studied as a rational, mechanical, causal structure, the historical development of which can be understood as *"the process of the ever more ingenious, expansive, and differentiated mastery of sound material in its objective possibilities for structural ties"*.[61]

---

57   Ibid., p. 38.

58   *Průmysl a technika v novodobé české kultuře: [sborník sympozia pořádaného Ústavem teorie a dějin umění ČSAV ve spolupráci s Národní galerií v Praze v rámci Smetanovských dnů v Plzni ve dnech 14.-16. 3. 1985.]* Praha: Ústav teorie a dějin umění Československé akademie věd, 1988.

59   HANSLICK, Eduard. *Vom Musikalisch-Schönen: ein Beitrag zur Revision der Ästhetik der Tonkunst*, 1854. 3. verbesserte Aufl. Leipzig: Rudolph Weigel, 1865.

60   HELMHOLTZ, Hermann von. *Die Lehre von den Tonempfindungen als physiologische Grundlage für die Theorie der Musik.* Vieweg, 1965.

61   VOJTĚCH, Ivan. Technika a hudební senzibilita. In *Průmysl a technika v novodobé české kultuře*, op. cit., 1988.

There is also discussion of the terms "simultaneity", "synaesthesia", and "spatialism", which se are now able to express using the term "multimedia".[62] Vojtěch's essay concludes with a reference to E. A. Poe and his essay *The Philosophy of Composition* (1846), on the basis of which he understands the arts as the relationship between mathematical construction and a creative metaphorical mode, i.e. the relationship between a calculable rational structure and the field of living meanings. As an example, he discusses *Poème électronique* (1958) by Edgard Varèse and Le Corbusier, in which individual metaphorical fields in the character of multimedia are inserted into the rationally conceived structure of the whole work.

Another comprehensive area of research on the relationship between music and technology is the question of **music and the media**. There has been ongoing research on the topic in this country since the 1990s, when as part of the project TEMPUS Music Media Training Programme for the Czech Republic, Jiří Fukač led the collective creation of the monograph *Hudba a média: rukověť muzikologa*[63] (Music and Media: A Manual for the Musicologist), which used the help of institutional "insiders" to map out the practice of dominant mass media of the day (radio and television). In theoretical matters, it mainly built upon the sociological research of Th. W. Adorno, W. Benjamin, K. Blaukopf, and V. Karbusický and the philosophical studies of M. McLuhan, V. Flusser, J.-F. Lyotard et al.

A newer contribution to the local discussion of the relationship between technology (the media) and the arts (including music) is *Umění a nová média*[64] (The Arts and the New Media), a collective monograph of four authors that was created in the environment of the Department of Musicology of the Masaryk University. Indicative of the enormous interest in this question in Czech academia is the fact that the publication and its second printing were sold out within just a few years.

In recent years, the question of the relationship between music and technology has been dealt with in the greatest breadth by the Centre for Basic Research of the Academy of Performing Arts in Prague and Masaryk University in Brno in "Výzkum funkcí techniky při vzniku a provozování múzického díla" (Research on the Function of Technology in the Creation and Performance in the Performing Arts), which was active from 2005 to 2008. The basic focal point of the research was:

> "[...] the standing and role of technology (from technikos to techne in relation to poiesis, or to invention and imagination) in artistic practice in general and its influence on the form of artistic activities and on the reception and dissemination of their products in a media-oriented society. This involves the study of this question at all levels, beginning with the level of the relationship of artistic creation and craftsmanship (poiesis–techne, ingenium–ars), including the relationship between the 'innate' and the 'teachable', and

---

62   "A multimedium is a type of media composed of autonomous media, which acquire new meaning in the context of a defined whole." FLAŠAR, Martin. Hudba v kontextu multimédií. In FLAŠAR, M., HORÁKOVÁ, J. and MACEK, P. (eds.). *Umění a nová média*. Brno: Masarykova univerzita, 2011, p. 36.

63   FUKAČ, Jiří and MACEK, Petr. *Hudba a média: rukověť muzikologa*. Brno: Masarykova univerzita, 1998.

64   FLAŠAR, M., HORÁKOVÁ, J. and MACEK, P. (eds.), op. cit., 2011.

continuing on the level of the relationship between the arts and technology understood as a tool (e.g. a musical instrument or the lighting equipment in a theatre) and a 'medium' (using electronic and digital technology), then proceeding to the level of dissemination, i.e. the problem of reproducibility and questions of the societal standing of audiovisual culture, i.e. the question of expression and communication at the level of artistic production, entertainment, and contemplation at the level of perception and reception, originality, and reproducibility."[65]

A particular weakness of the whole project was the breadth of its scope because it encompassed research in the areas of theatre, the audio-visual arts, and music. Therefore, it was more valuable for the scope of the issue that was covered than for the depth of the investigation of the individual arts. In terms of the outcomes, music was represented relatively marginally in narrow topics (such as the relationship between operetta and musicals). For this reason, the project as such was not very helpful with respect to the issue we are investigating.

Film music, video game music, and specific types of music with a heteronomous function account for a special domain of cognitive reflection on music and sound in the media. These types of music were long neglected by musicology or were cautiously bypassed. The main problem was the traditional understanding of music as a self-contained artwork that can be analysed formally or structurally, with overlaps into aesthetic or artistic value judgments. Of course, the realm of functional music raises quite different questions. It deals primarily with questions of the dramaturgy of sound/music within a whole consisting of multiple media (intermedia, multimedia), questions of musical psychology and psychoacoustics (working with emotions, manipulative/persuasive techniques etc.), new forms of structuring sound and music in time and space (especially in video game music, sound as a part of interactive/responsive systems etc.). Another heretofore relatively neglected field is the sphere of the perception of music involving sociological research of audiences and their behaviour (not only in concert halls and theatres or on radio and television, but also in public places). Especially in the field of game studies, sound and music participate to the fullest extent not only in constructing communicated meaning (like in film), but also in the structuring of spacetime, strengthening the player's immersion and flow.

Further literature must be sought in categories like electroacoustic music, sound art, radio art, film music, video game music etc. At that level, we find historically well-developed discourses with their own communities of experts and established publication channels. Most of the publications are articles in journals and separately published studies. Books written in Czech reflecting on the theory, aesthetics, and history of these categories are found only sporadically, and the number of them in the past century is numbered in the single digits rather than in dozens.

---

65   Výroční zpráva Centra základního výzkumu AMU a MU [online]. [Accessed on 10 July 2017]. Retrieved from: https://www.amu.cz/cs/ovvp/msmt/programy-podpory-vav/centra-zakladniho-vyzkumu/dokumentace/vyrocni-zprava-centra-zakladniho-vyzkumu-amu-mu-za-rok-2005.

It is for the most part practically oriented creators, i.e. academically active composers and musicians, who exhibit the strongest motivation toward cognitive reflection in the area of musical technologies. From among the latest studies in this area, we should mention at least the theoretical work being done at the Janáček Academy of Performing Arts in Brno and at the Academy of Performing Arts in Prague. In the case of the academy in Brno, there are texts by Ivo Medek devoted to multimedia, tying in with the work of Piňos (e.g. the study *Multimediální dílo – teorie a praxe* written jointly with Markéta Dvořáková)[66] or the habilitation thesis by Dan Dlouhý (*Počítačem podporovaná algoritmická kompozice*).[67] In the case of the Academy of Performing Arts in Prague, there is the work of Michal Rataj and his students (e.g. *Digitální technologie v hudební tvorbě pro akustické nástroje*).[68]

Traditionally, musicology has been very lacking in studies taking a synthesising approach capable of overcoming the boundaries between the individual lower categories and aiming higher, towards more universally applicable conclusions and theories. We occasionally find this ability, usually among those whose primary focus is not musicology. The most valuable observations of this kind are found in the areas of philosophy, sociology, or aesthetics. The situation is apparently caused by the unwillingness of analytically and narrowly oriented musicologists to stand back from the sum of details and to seek a higher perspective on the entire question. Detailed knowledge is certainly of key importance, but only in the context of a real understanding of the whole. One may justifiably assume that it is the constantly increasing degree of specialisation in musicology that makes it difficult to see things as a whole and that also hinders the communication of experts with the broader public. One must therefore appreciate the transverse perspectives of those who are not up to their waists in details and are capable of perceiving interconnections of phenomena cutting across rigid categories. They are working with a number of such perspectives in case studies.

A real problem for studying the area of relationships between music and technology is its character as a "buffer zone". This seldom-conquered territory lies between the areas of external etic approaches of non-musicologists (philosophers, sociologists, aestheticians, psychologists etc.) and emic approaches of musicologists limited by the internal methodologies of their own field.

---

66   In FLAŠAR, M., HORÁKOVÁ, J. and MACEK, P. (eds.), op. cit., 2011.

67   DLOUHÝ, Dan. *Počítačem podporovaná algoritmická kompozice* [habilitation thesis]. Brno: JAMU, 2013.

68   RATAJ, Jakub and AGOSTINHO, Gilberto. *Digitální technologie v hudební tvorbě pro akustické nástroje.* Praha: AMU, 2016.

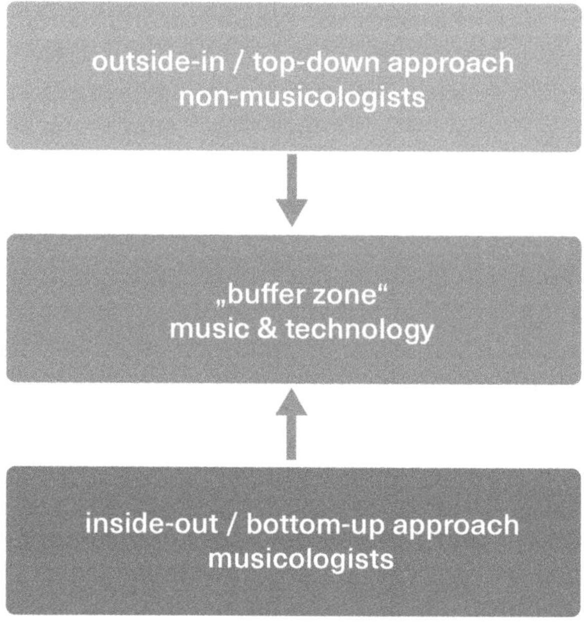

Fig. 4 Music and technology as a methodological "buffer zone".

With some simplification, one might say that the sparsely populated interdisciplinary realm of the topic "music and technology" has been colonised on the one hand by intellectual adventurers with too universal a focus and on the other hand by those whose specialisation is too narrow. Another option could be a division between traditionally oriented musicology and the practice of new music avoiding musicology.

1.4 Assumptions and objectives

This book is the outcome of long-term study and cognitive reflection on the musical thinking of elite representatives of Euro-American art music of the 20th and 21st centuries. On the one hand, there are the theoretically formulated poetics, and on the other hand there is the musical creation itself. Usually, the two worlds are interconnected because all composers are intellectuals who are continually reflecting theoretically upon their works.

The most important goal of this publication is clearly to present a synthesising study on the relationship between technologies and contemporary musical creation, something that has heretofore been lacking in Czech musicology. Through interpretations and case studies of the thinking of specific composers, we shall attempt the abstracting of basic concepts that appear to be dominant in this discourse. On their basis, we shall attempt to put together a synthesising picture of technologically supported music, in which we shall attempt to identify more general tendencies and strategies.

What are the hypotheses with which we will be approaching the topic?

— **One may reasonably assume that electronic technologies and the breakneck pace of development in that field have radically changed the musical thinking of the 20ᵗʰ and 21ˢᵗ centuries.** The source of this assumption is the emergence of independent schools and types of music and media arts (e.g. electroacoustic music, radio art, sound art, sound-based music, minimalist music etc.). This study will raise not only pragmatic questions like "how?", but also ontological questions like "why?".

— **The electrification and digitisation of music have led to the redefining or calling into question of the function and nature of authorship, musical instrument, interpretation, and the originality of an artwork.** In other words, it seems clear that the nature of encoding of a musical work has changed the whole process of musical communication and its basic components. The chapters that follow will be devoted to the causes and characteristics of those changes.

— **Efforts to make creative use of new technologies have been caused by both external and internal factors.** External causes involve in particular the calls of European philosophers for the humanisation of technology in connection with the idea of technological determinism, where internal causes are represented primarily by the musicians' own recognition of the experimental and innovative potential of technologies for new music. We shall attempt to examine these causes both in the context of established discourses and by analyses of concrete manifestations of musical thinking.

— **Musical thinking reacts sensitively to changes of thinking, society, and technology, so these changes should be reflected in the music itself.** Despite the ideas of New Musicology expressed by Joseph Kerman in his essay *How We Got into Analysis, and How to Get Out,*[69] we still believe in accordance with Helfert's conviction that without understanding of musical structure, it is not possible to understand correctly an individual musical thought or the form of musical style arising from it. We shall therefore attempt to point out parallels between individual musical ideas and general period thinking on technologies.

— **Just as intellectual stances towards technologies have undergone a shift in the course of the 20ᵗʰ and 21ˢᵗ centuries mainly in the direction of a critical attitude, we anticipate that we will find criticisms in the area of music**

69　KERMAN, Joseph. How We Got into Analysis, and How to Get Out. *Critical Inquiry*, Vol. 7, No. 2 (Winter, 1980), pp. 311–331 [online]. [Accessed on 29 Aug. 2018]. University of Chicago Press. Retrieved from: https://www.jstor.org/stable/1343130.

as well. Therefore, in the following text we will be monitoring the attitudes of musicians towards technologies ranging from utopian to critical conceptions of music.

— **Technology in music cannot be eliminated.** Or can it? Does music without technology exist? Is it at all possible to escape technical thinking when creating a musical artefact or process? What might or should post-technological music be like? These and other questions serve to open subsequent discussion.

Chapter 2

Music and Technology –
– Formulation of the Problem

The question of the relationship between music and technology is the question of the relationship between musical and technical (instrumental, utilitarian) thinking. As we said above, the function of mankind of from an anthropological perspective in this relationship cannot be ignored. To introduce the question, we will turn to the theses of Martin Heidegger, which are becoming increasingly important as time goes by. When studying texts on the problem of technologically conditioned music, the reader will necessarily encounter his ideas sooner or later. Those ideas are still relevant and valuable because of the generality of the question, which is posed at an ontological level, is based on the historical analysis of the term, and offers a broad range of possible use. Moreover, the author addressed the world of the arts directly. His proposal must therefore be accepted as a challenged for opening the question.

2.1 Heidegger's proposal

> "Because the essence of technology is nothing technological, essential reflection upon technology and decisive confrontation with it must happen in a realm that is, on the one hand, akin to the essence of technology and, on the other, fundamentally different from it. Such a realm is art."
>
> Martin Heidegger: *The Question Concerning Technology*[70]

To clarify the purpose of this book, it should at least be said that it is an attempt to answer a question raised more than 60 years ago by the philosopher Martin Heidegger in his lecture *Die Frage nach der Technik* that was part of a cycle of lectures titled *The Arts in the Technological Age*. The question he raised seems to be relatively banal: "What is technology?". For that, the hidden depths into which he takes his arguments seem all the more surprising and remote.

---

70   HEIDEGGER, M. *The Question Concerning Technology and Other Essays*, op. cit., p. 35.

In his intellectually provocative text *Rules for the Human Zoo*,[71] Peter Sloterdijk compares philosophy to a chain letter not addressed to a specific person, with copyists and scribes joining in who feel themselves to have a calling for such activity or are simply enchanted and attracted by it. Our motivation for dealing with Heidegger's text belongs more under the second category mentioned.

In surveying the boundaries of the problem, Heidegger's point of departure is the careful analysis of the word *technology* because language and the ways we talk about things are an expression of our thinking about them. In interpretations of the meanings of that word, he finds connections with other words like *knowing* (*epistēmē*) or creating (*poiēsis*).

> "[we ask] what the name 'technology' means. The word stems from the Greek. *Technikon* means that which belongs to *technē*. We must observe two things with respect to the meaning of this word. One is that *technē* is the name not only for the activities and skills of the craftsman, but also for the arts of the mind and the fine arts. *Technē* belongs to bringing-forth, to *poiēsis*; it is something poietic.
>
> The other point that we should observe with regard to *technē* is even more important. From earliest times until Plato the word *technē* is linked with the word *epistēmē*. Both words are names for knowing in the widest sense. They mean to be entirely at home in something, to understand and be expert in it."[72]

According to Heidegger, *technē* has an essential connection to the discovery of truth and beauty. The implications of the word *technē* or *technology* belong to the realm of ethics and aesthetics, thence also their relationship with the arts.

> "And the *poiēsis* of the fine arts also was called technē. In Greece, at the outset of the destining of the West, the arts soared to the supreme height of the revealing granted them. [...] And art was simply called *technē*. It was a single, manifold revealing. It was pious, *promos*, i.e., yielding to the holding-sway and the safekeeping of truth. The arts were not derived from the artistic. Art works were not enjoyed aesthetically. Art was not a sector of cultural activity."[73]

Notice the last sentences of the quote. We can read them in reverse as a statement that is critical of the present state of the arts, which is artificial (i.e. synthetic, engineered, affected, overly refined, detached etc.) and serves for aesthetic pleasure within the context of cultural activity or a culture industry (T. W. Adorno, M. Horkheimer). At the same time, Heidegger seems to see the arts as losing their aura of truthfulness and identification with reality.

---

71   SLOTERDIJK, Peter. *Regeln für den Menschenpark. Ein Antwortschreiben zu Heideggers Brief über den Humanismus.* Sonderdruck. Edition Suhrkamp: Frankfurt am Main, 1999.

72   HEIDEGGER, op. cit., pp. 12–13.

73   Ibid., p. 34.

"What, then, was art—perhaps only for that brief but magnificent time? Why did art bear the modest name *technē*? Because it was a revealing that brought forth and hither, and therefore belonged within *poiēsis*. It was finally that revealing which holds complete sway in all the fine arts, in poetry, and in everything poetical that obtained *poiēsis* as its proper name."[74]

Thus, the word *technē* is synonymous with *art*. There is no difference between technology and art from an etymological perspective. Historically, art was long understood instrumentally, i.e. as a mere means of means of revealing and discovering goodness and truth. Heidegger understands technology both as a set of resources and as the needs and purposes for which they serve. Therefore, the purpose of technology is exclusively instrumental, and one must take great care that it does not deviate from that purpose. The 20th and 21st centuries face the confusing of means and ends. Technology often improperly shifts from being a mere resource to the position of the goal of human reasoning and striving.

"Everything depends on our manipulating technology in the proper manner as a means. We will, as we say, get technology 'spiritually in hand.' We will master it. The will to mastery becomes all the more urgent the more technology threatens to slip from human control."[75]

Heidegger's message is comprehensible. There is no abstract "technology". Technology is just a set of resources and procedures used and practised by mankind. In his text, Heidegger—apparently deliberately—does not discuss mankind, whose absence from the text is provocative, and that might be the author's hidden message. Heidegger says technology needs to be kept in its place as a tool that serves for the creation of beauty and the discovery of truth, all under the control of the human mind, and not the other way around. From the rest of the lecture, it is clear that the German philosopher is not posing this problem as an abstract, analytical game, but as a relevant problem that he as a philosopher is trying to solve.

If we apply Heidegger's point of view to the question of the relationship between music and technology in the 20th and 21st centuries, our deliberations lead us to the key to unlocking the question. It represents a departure point for investigating the problem of the role of technologies in contemporary music. It asks how to establish a balance between the end and the means, i.e. between artistic expression and the technology or medium used, which component is dominant in the mutual, dynamic relationship, and in what cases the guiding principle is the artist's intent, or to the contrary, the nature of the technology being used. The text that follows intends to find answers to these questions. Therefore, the goal of our study is to examine and evaluate the extent to which Heidegger's task for the contemporary arts has been fulfilled successfully by artists.

---

74   Ibid., p. 34.

75   Ibid., p. 8.

2.2 Music, science, and technology

As we have shown, technique and technology also tend to be seen as the sphere of applications of the findings of science. Therefore, it is highly useful to consider the relationship of music to technology in the context of science.

In the past, the author of this book has devoted himself to the question of the relationship between music and the natural sciences in the chapter of *Hudba na křižovatkách umění a přírodních věd* (Music at the Intersections of the Arts and the Natural Sciences) of a collective monograph that studied the relationships between science and art at a general level.[76] Therefore, we will now only briefly touch upon some arguments and observations and attempt to supplement them with some more findings.

As an explanation of the relationship between music and the natural sciences, references are often made back to the medieval system of sciences, in which music belongs to the quadrivium alongside the other arts or the sciences of "pure reason": mathematics, geometry, and astronomy. Here, of course, music is not understood merely as a mere craft of production and interpretation, but rather as a rigorous science tightly bound to the laws of mathematics. To this day, mathematics and physics extend deeply into the field of music theory, and the study and understanding of music without them would not be possible. Like technology, music is an expression of rationality that manifests itself as various forms of arrangement of sound material. The English theoretical physicist and mathematician John D. Barrow expressed this fittingly in his book *The Artful Universe*, a remarkable synthesis of ideas:

"Where there is life there is a pattern, and where there is a pattern there is mathematics. Once that germ of rationality and order exists to turn a chaos into a cosmos, then so does mathematics."[77] Barrow is referring to a remark made by Igor Stravinsky: *"Music's exclusive function is to structure the flow of time and keep order in it ... music is the art of the permutation of time."*[78]

This idea is shared by the Czech music theorist and musicologist Vladimír Tichý in his study *Chaos a hudba* (Chaos and Music):

"One of the aesthetic ideals that both composers and performers of classical European music try to fulfil is striving for perfect form. There is no disputing that from both from an analytical perspective and purely based on listening to Bach's Art of the Fugue, one cannot help but admire the amazing, unequalled sense of order manifesting itself both in the whole and in every detail of the work and in the rich network of its internally organising relationships; in terms of compositional technique, the work is an example of the 'higher mathematics' of a composer's work. A similar tribute can be paid to works by Mozart, Beethoven, Brahms..."[79]

---

76 GIBODA, Michal (ed.). *Mosty a propasti mezi vědou a uměním*. České Budějovice: Občanské sdružení Dialog vědy s uměním, 2010.

77 BARROW, John D. *The Artful Universe*. Oxford University Press, 1995, p. 230.

78 Ibid., p. 193.

79 TICHÝ, Vladimír. Chaos a hudba. In *Živá hudba XIV: sborník prací Hudební fakulty Akademie múzických umění*. Praha: Státní pedagogické nakladatelství, 2005, p. 152.

In its rational complexity, music is inseparable from the arts, the humanities, and the natural sciences. It is, in fact, both a rational and an emotional arrangement of acoustical phenomena in strictly structured time and space. For this reason, it embodies a number of dichotomies, from objective existence to the subjective, and from the rational to the emotional. Therefore, it can also be studied using scientific methods that we classify among the natural sciences (physics, mathematics) or among the humanities or social sciences (history, sociology).

While order had been understood since ancient times as the opposite of chaos or as a means of taming chaos, in the 20th century chaos began to attract the attention of not only mathematicians and physicists (Werner Heisenberg postulated the uncertainty principle in 1927, and Edward Lorenz began devoting himself to non-linear dynamical systems in the early 1960s), but also artists. Geometrical regularity and determinism of musical structure give way to elements that are disruptive and call the structure into doubt. There was a turn away from traditional harmony based upon simple ratios of regularly vibrating bodies, the tone as the basic unit of musical structure gave way to noise (the result of irregular vibration), and the regular geometry of form corresponding to duple or triple meter etc. was broken up. The ideas of unpredictability, indefiniteness, and probability appeared in the music of the latter half of the 20th century with John Cage (indeterminacy), Pierre Boulez (aleatory), and Iannis Xenakis (stochastic music).

2.3 Two models for the coexistence of science and the arts

If the arts and science are just two different forms of learning about the world, the place where the interaction between them takes place is the human subject. From the standpoint of the relationship between mankind and the arts, on the basis of empirical experiences we can propose two models for the mutual coexistence of science and the arts: the model of integration and the model of cooperation. While the former is individualistic (intrapersonal), the latter is cooperative (interpersonal).

The individualistic Renaissance ideal combining imagination and technical skill with the methodical rationality of a scientist in a single person began to seem less and less possible from a certain level of development and specialisation in the sciences. Leonardo da Vinci tends in general to be regarded as an example of the quasi-mythical embodiment of this ideal type of artist-thinker. In his approach to reality, the transfer of knowledge, skill, and experience could take place with absolute freedom. The integrated model for the coexistence of the sciences and arts in the mind of a single human individual, still operative in the mid-17th century (see e.g. *Musurgia universalis* by Athanasius Kircher, 1650), definitively disintegrated in the latter half of the 18th century into a plethora of disparate fields of human knowledge and of the arts under the strict scrutiny of the French Encyclopaedists and other figures of the Enlightenment. From that moment onwards, examples of the universal scientist-artist type have become a rather exceptional phenomenon.

We find the cooperative model in the 20th century wherever the lines of science (and technology) intersect with lines of the arts. The deepening of individual scientific fields and their further splitting into new subdisciplines necessarily led to the existence of experts specialising in a narrow slice of a field of knowledge. The transfer of acquired knowledge between individual fields is secured by interpersonal and interdisciplinary communication. The same also applies to communication between representatives of the arts and of science. Without their close cooperation, many key projects and concepts would not have been realised. Symptomatic of this new model of collaboration was the period after the Second World War, when the newly emerging artworks would have been unthinkable without the scientists or technical experts who were masters of the latest technologies. The 20th century was a century of wars, which became the catalyst for the development of technologies. Paradoxically, it is to warfare that we are "indebted" for the development of radio, satellite communications, recording media, and the internet. Just as the tape recorder was the child of the Second World War, the internet is a product of the Cold War. The magnetic tape and the possibilities it offers for the manipulation of sound such as changes of speed, modulation, reversal etc. enabled the creation of new studies of electronic music in Europe and overseas, but the work done in that field would have been unthinkable without the cooperation of scientists and artists. The former had a perfect understanding and mastery of the technology, but they were unable to make creative use of it at a higher level, while the latter had artistic ambitions and intentions, but they were unable to use the new tools efficiently to achieve their goals. The first studio of this kind, Studio d'Essai in Paris, was established through the cooperation of the engineer Pierre Schaeffer and the composer Pierre Henry. Likewise, the Westdeutscher Rundfunk Electronic Music Studio in Cologne could not have operated without cooperation between Herbert Eimert and Karlheinz Stockhausen. This led to the division of the creative process between an artist (author of the work's concept) and a technician (who realises the project). It was not until later, when artists gained technical experience and skills and when, at the same time, technologies became simpler, that there was a convergence of the arts and technology into a single, integrated, subjective whole.

Chapter 3

Music from the Perspective of Technology

3.1 Mankind and the musical instrument (or machine)

The subject matter of the following chapters will be an investigation of the function of machines in music ranging from music for which mankind is the benchmark to music that is created technologically.

We find many examples of interactions of mechanical, chemical, or electronic technologies with the arts from the 19th century onwards. Beginning with the daguerreotype process and continuing with film, radio, television, sound recording, and data storage media and ending (for now) with the internet, we see in all of these and other media the possibility for integration of science-conditioned form and its potentially aesthetic content.

> "Today man has developed extensions for practically everything he used to do with his body. The evolution of weapons begins with the teeth and the fist and ends with the atom bomb. Clothes and houses are extensions of man's biological temperature-control mechanisms. Furniture takes the place of squatting and sitting on the ground. Power tools, glasses, TV, telephones, and books which carry the voice across both time and space are examples of material extensions. Money is a way of extending and storing labor. Our transportation networks now do what we used to do with our feet and backs. In fact, all man-made material things can be treated as extensions of what man once did with his body or some specialized part of his body."[80]

This quote, which inspired Marshall McLuhan to create his well-known diagram in which the media appear in the role of extensions of the human senses, can be applied successfully to any technology including musical instruments. In the areas of the construction of instruments, discoveries from acoustics, materials physics etc. were being employed to an unprecedented extent. Just as human beings determined the nature and the function of their extensions, these extensions in

---

80   HALL, Edward T. *The Silent Language*. Doubleday & Company, Inc., Garden City, New York, 1959, p. 79.

turn predetermined the behaviour of their users. Music and the forms it has taken have always been determined primarily by the possibilities of musical instruments, such as their range of frequencies, their flexibility (enabling the quick alternation of tones of the same or different frequencies), or their dynamic ranges, which were bound to the acoustic properties of the performance space (church, concert hall, salon, music hall, stadium etc.). The connection between the player and the musical instrument is so close that their aspects become intertwined. For example, violinists insistently maintain that it takes some time to "break in" a new violin. In reality, no change to the wood's structure has ever been proven, and the phenomenon is simply the player's psychomotor system adapting to a new instrument. Should we be afraid of the changes that await us when we come into contact with new technologies serving for the production of music? Undoubtedly, every new instrument or new technology introduces new ways of thinking to music. McLuhan quotes an ancient Chinese story, in which the sage Tsu-Gung discusses the dangers that tools or machines can represent for a person:

> "[...] whoever uses machines does all his work like a machine. He who does his work like a machine grows a heart like a machine, and he who carries the heart of a machine in his breast loses his simplicity. He who has lost his simplicity becomes unsure in the strivings of his soul. Uncertainty in the strivings of the soul is something which does not agree with honest sense. It is not that I do not know of such things; I am ashamed to use them."[81]

The meaning of this brief story is clear: technologies and their functions foist upon users their own logic and determine how they will think and act. We might view technologies as a potential tool for dehumanisation and objectivization. Of course, this scepticism is just one of the possible attitudes towards technologies.

Igor Stravinsky, for example, takes a more conciliatory stance towards technology as an objective principle. In his Harvard lectures from 1938–39, he discusses the utility and even necessity of restrictive measures (objective obstacles and limits) that the composer must impose on himself in the infinite universe of music in order to create something meaningful within that framework.[82] Likewise, in Stravinsky's (reflective and musical) thinking, we find a number of efforts to find a balance between the mechanical (artificial) and the human (natural) principle in music. Examples include his pragmatic interest in the mechanical player piano or the rhythmic-mechanical role assigned to the piano and strings in his compositions. Stravinsky compensates for these mechanical principles by his interest in folklore, folk traditions, fairy tales etc. The things he had to say about Edgard Varèse as a composer who managed to adjust the limits between the

---

81 MCLUHAN, Marshall. *Understanding Media: The Extensions of Man*, GINGKO PRESS Inc., Berkeley, California, 2013, p. 64.

82 STRAVINSKY, Igor. *Poetics of Music in the Form of Six Lextures*. Translated by Arthur Knodel and Ingolf Dahl. Cambridge: Harvard University Press, 1947.

mechanical and the human principle in music are evidence of Stravinsky's thinking along these lines.[83]

Umberto Eco also took a techno-optimistic, "comforting" stance towards the feared "musical machines". The period of his life he spent working at RAI in Milan, home of one of Europe's leading electronic music studios (Studio di fonologia musicale RAI di Milano) entitled him to make such a defence. Eco rejected the superficial societal criticism of mechanically produced music, pointing out that all music other than vocal music had long been produced exclusively by machines.[84] He saw the relationship between technology and its user as the key to evaluating the role of technology in musical culture. He refuted the widespread concern that the new technologies were too complex to be humanised:

> "[it] is not the complexity of equipment that influences the possibility of 'humanising' one instrument or another, so it is quite possible to imagine a musician who composes a series of tones manufactured and assembled with the help of electronic instruments and equipment and who, in turn, knows the nature of his instrument so perfectly that when facing its panel, he behaves like a pianist at the keyboard."[85]

He furthermore points out that the arts have been working with concept of technology since ancient times. Techniques or technologies are nothing more than a set of ways of manipulating the material with which the artform in question is working, and rather than being an obstacle, technology can become a kind of guide, a necessary condition, a limit, which determines the creative artist's possibilities. In this sense, Eco understands technology as a positive factor that can inspire or positively stimulate artists.

Let us now examine the three previous attitudes from our own perspective. If an instrument (or machine) is the result of creative human thought, how could it impose its own logic on a person? There is nothing else to say about musical instruments (or machines) either. The relationship between a human and an instrument is interactive; both parts of a closed system influence each other. Playing a musical instrument might make a person's behaviour mechanical in the sense of the accepting of the instrument's principles of construction (the keyboard mechanism, the keys and valves of wind instruments etc.), but in turn it provides the player with the possibility of organising complex sound structures in time and space. That magical experience draws a person out of his everyday life and routine. In a world, which itself operates like a machine,[86] a musical instrument is a means of taking a person away from the immediate reality of living, a means of the free creative realisation of individuality, and at the same time a unique factor of shared experiencing and of the creating of shared culture. The use of musical instruments (or machines) takes us

---

83   STRAVINSKIJ, Igor and CRAFT, Robert. *Dialogues and A Diary.* Doubleday & Company, 1963, p. 59.

84   ECO, Umberto. *Apocalittici e integrati.* Milano: Bompiani, 1994. Chapter *La musica et la macchina.*

85   Ibid., p. 322.

86   Cf. ORTEGA Y GASSET, José, op. cit., 2011, p. 41.

full circle back to the human being, regardless of whether what is involves is a violin, piano, synthesizer, laptop computer, or printed circuit board amplifier. As Herbert Marcuse wrote:

> "The 'high culture' [...] has its own rites and its own style. The salon, the concert, opera, theatre are designed to create and invoke another dimension of reality. Their attendance requires festive-like preparation; they cut off and transcend everyday experience."[87]

According to him, the power of the arts lies in the rational negation of everyday life. In this process, musical instruments can become a rational means of stepping out of everyday life. For a further interpretation, one must try to define the boundary between music produced by a human and music produced purely technologically.

Music produced by people (singing, playing an instrument) is based on their psycho-motoric dispositions. Because a human engaged in musical activity is creating a unity of production and perception, the music takes shape as the result of the extent of a person's ability to move (speed of finger movements, breathing, muscular activity of the vocal cords etc.) as well as of the ability to use the ear to make corrections within a certain amount of time. Other factors include concentration, mental and physical condition etc. From this point of view, humans are very flexible, but individuals are limited by various factors. They are relatively weak (with respect to the exerting of force), unreliable (fallible), imprecise in the placement of sound events in time and space (e.g. by touching a string), and ill-suited to repetitive activity for long periods of time.

Let us now examine the basic components of music that are determined by the limitations of the human body:

1. kinetic: rhythm and tempo – depends on psychomotoric disposition,
2. melodic – given by a person's vocal range, capability of the vocal cords,
3. harmonic – a person can sing only one note at a time,
4. dynamic – combination of breathing and vocal cords,
5. colour (spectral composition of sound) – combination of the positioning of the internal parts of the head and the generation of tone,
6. structural (form and structure) – given by the possibilities of human memory,
7. spatial – bound to the physical movement of a human being in space.

Until the 19th century, music was the music of a human being, or to be more precise, a reflection of a human being's biological capabilities. In particular, music's range of tones and tempos was based on the limitations of the human body. Even in instrumental music, the range of tones stayed within the range reproducible by the human voice. Therefore, music has mostly been based historically on the frequencies of physiological processes: musical tempos respect the usual range of

---

87   MARCUSE, Herbert. *One-Dimensional Man. Studies in the Ideology of Advanced Industrial Society.* Boston: Beacon Press, 1966, pp. 63–64.

pulse frequencies (at least approximately: lento or largo represent the speed of ca. 40–60 beats per minute, which is the at-rest pulse rate of a person in peak physical condition, while prestissimo is about 200 beats per minute, which is the maximum heart rate of an 18-year-old male), a person's rate of motion (andante from the Italian word "andare" – to walk, etc.), or functional capacity (the tempo of a vocal phrase based on the human lung capacity).

As opposed to music defined by the dispositions of the human body, at the turn of the 18th and 19th centuries, there was a second type of music that was defining itself in reaction to the development of machines. Let us recall a machine's general characteristics:

1. a machine's performance has a specifically defined function and goal;
2. it is precise and does not make mistakes;
3. if necessary, it is as fast as possible;
4. its strength exceeds the limitations of the human body;
5. it has great endurance and reliability – it is capable of a large number of repetitions while maintaining a constantly high level of quality of production;
6. economical – guarantees a suitable level of profit relative to costs.

The musical automatons of the 18th century, in a sense the first musical machines, were a peculiar fusion of music as a typical musical activity with the newly emerging technical thinking of the mechanical era. In Europe of the modern age, we have records of musical androids like the flute player made by Jacques de Vaucanson (1738–41), which was 188 cm tall and could play 12 songs, a female android playing the organ made by the Swiss watchmaker Henri Droz (1773), and a horseman made by watchmaker Petr Heinrich, from Prague's Lesser Town, which is said to have galloped and trotted and could be made to play 12 trumpet melodies by pressing various body parts. Mechanical musical figurines even became a line of business, as in the case of the "mechanical artists" made by Jakob and Karl Sachatzek, who presented a performance by a mechanical trumpeter, drummer, tympanist, and even a mechanical tightrope walker at the Reduta in Brno on 5 November 1810.[88]

Especially characteristic of the early 19th century was the development of such autonomous mechanical instruments as the harmonichord, the physharmonica, the salpingion, the chordaulodion, and the symphonion.

Mechanical characteristics projected onto live musical performing appear soon after the arrival of the first industrial revolution in the phenomenon of virtuosity. Etymologically, the words "virtuosity" and "virtuoso" are derived from Latin:

vir – man;
virtus – perfection, virtue;
virtuosus – good, virtuous, perfect.

---

88   Jan Trojan has dealt with this topic in more detail in his study Mechanicko-muzikální umělecké figuríny aneb O neuvěřitelných zážitcích ve staré brněnské Redutě. *Opus musicum*, 2005, 4, pp. 4–8.

Fig. 5 Detail from a theatrical poster promoting a performance by mechanical figurines. J. and K. Sachatzek in Brno (1810). *Opus musicum*, 2005, 4, p. 4.

The term "virtuoso" appears at the turn of the 17th and 18th centuries, and it refers to a solo artist (basically exclusively a man in those days) armed with interpretive perfection. In the 19th century, Franz Liszt and Frédéric Chopin understood very well that the bourgeois public demanded of performers something extraordinary, marvellous, and mechanical, and that while virtuosity was not the goal of music, it was definitely an essential part of it.[89] A virtuoso presents himself to the public as a person called by God to disseminate the Arts. With the growing mass scale of the institution of the public bourgeois concert, there was an increasing emphasis on secondary features of musical interpretation like speed, accuracy, endurance, range of abilities etc. The bourgeoisie thus created a greater demand for sensation, performance, and competitiveness, bringing the arts closer to sports, acrobatics, and juggling, as T. W. Adorno noted.[90] The period phenomena of geniuses or prodigies fit well in this schema, as did the newly emerging phenomenon of the star who becomes a projection of the unfulfilled wishes and desires of the public and a model for a lifestyle worthy of following.

In the process of virtuosity, we find a shift of emphasis from the autonomous artistic (aesthetic) function of music to the technical aspect of its interpretation. And more importantly, music in the age of virtuosity begins to be composed for external effect, i.e. for the exhibition of the player's technique instead of for expressing the composer's internally felt artistic intent. There is a shift of priority away from the musical work and towards the interpretation and its reception. Composed music becomes a means of presenting technique, with technique now coming before the

---

89   Cf. ADORNO, Theodor W. *Schéma masové kultury* [Das Schema der Massenkultur. Kulturindustrie (Fortsetzung)]. Praha: Oikoymenh, 2009, pp. 47–49.

90   Ibid.

creation of the music because it makes structural demands on what the music will be like. In the process of composing, composers try to take into account or even accentuate the technical strengths of the performer or, if the composers is also the performers, they try to show off their technical strengths and hide their weaknesses. One might say that in this case, technique is both the cause and the destination of the music. There are many examples of virtuosic compositions of the 19th and 20th centuries such as Niccolò Paganini's *24 Caprices*, Franz Liszt's piano etudes etc. The actual genre of the etude in the 19th century is actually the exercising of a specific technical skill, and it does not necessarily signify a high degree of artistic value.

As Filip Johánek points out in his study *Vztah technologie a rytmu v hudbě 20. a 21. století* (The Relationship between Technology and Rhythm in the Music of the 20th and 21st Centuries), according to Herbert Marcuse, technique becomes the common denominator of various cultural forms:

> "The choice of the historical alternative of the machine as an instrument for mastery of nature thus begins to be the dominant factor in the development of society. This total tendency begins to infiltrate the worlds of language, behaviour, and spiritual and material culture; it subdues these worlds and begins to shape them. All of society's particularities— economics, politics (in the sense of political programmes), culture etc.—merge into a single medium, technology."[91]

If we consider music from the perspective of dynamics or volume of sound, we see in the 19th century an unambiguous tendency towards the strengthening of the sound of individual instruments and of the orchestra, reaching its height in the sound of the Romantic symphony orchestra of Wagner, Mahler, and Strauss at a time when the industrial era in Europe was reaching its climax and machines were bringing noise into the world of experience. Luigi Russolo describes this situation in his manifesto *L'Arte dei rumori* (The Art of Noise, 1913), taking a radical aesthetic turn on that basis. What, then are the aesthetic and structural consequences that the mechanical era brings to music? Primarily, they are as follows:

1. the principle of repetition – ostinato, motor rhythm;
2. emphasis on speed – fast tempos and speed of motion (figuration);
3. emphasis on regularity of motion – elimination of Romantic agogics;
4. insensitivity, objectivity – application of compositional and performance techniques;
5. dynamics – exploring possible limits of volume of instruments or the orchestra.

---

91   MARCUSE, Herbert. *One-Dimensional Man: Studies in the Ideology of Advanced Industrial Society.* London: Routledge, 2002, quoted in JOHÁNEK, Filip. *Vztah technologie a rytmu v hudbě 20. a 21. století.* Master's thesis. Supervisor: PhDr. Martin Flašar, Ph.D. Brno: Masarykova univerzita, 2014, p. 22.

3.2 Technology as a principle of objective music

In his essay *Hudba a hluk* (Music and Noise),[92] Milan Kundera writes about the beauty of objective music that is not burdened with false sentimentality. If we develop Kundera's idea further, we can regard music as objective when it delegates responsibility for the work's resultant form outside of the subject of the author, such as some kind of natural or technical (statistical, algorithmic, combinatorial) formal principle like chance, crystallisation, a mechanical or genetic principle etc. Of course, objectivity is also paradoxically a criterion that combines seemingly opposite compositional strategies like aleatory with the strict determinism of serialism. Both in fact arrive at highly complex structures.

Marcus Zagorski's book *Kapitoly z estetiky seriálnej hudby* (Chapters from the Aesthetics of Serial Music)[93] offers a relatively fresh perspective for understanding objectivity and subjectivity in the music of the 20th century. He devotes the second chapter to "Materialdenken", which permeates the aesthetics of the Darmstadt School at the turn of the 1950s and '60s. Zagorski notices that both the apologists for and critics of serialism join with T. W. Adorno in evoking the "tendency of the material" towards serial organisation, which they claim arises logically from Schoenberg's dodecaphony. They understand the entire situation of the development of serial music in a Hegelian manner as the consequence of the effect of the objective spirit of history. It was as if it were a matter of logical historical necessity that cannot be called into question by the consideration of the consensual orientation of several leading individual composers at the forefront of New Music. Carl Dahlhaus evaluated the entire situation retrospectively in 1982. He wrote that whenever the material seemingly showed the way the composers were supposed to be heading, what was actually at work was subjectivity that could not be concealed behind a façade of historical unavoidability.[94]

This hunger for objectivity was paradoxically caused by composers' attempts to escape the historicity of music by seeking new, historically unconditioned material. Zagorski finds the origin of this turning towards material with Adorno, who was incapable of resolving his (own personal) problem with Schoenberg and Stravinsky on a formal level because both used historical forms in their works. There was nothing left to do but to orient oneself towards the content or material, although in Schoenberg's case what is involved is more of a method than material. We should note that even Adorno's own entire historically objective construction had a simple and purely subjective cause, namely his opposition to Stravinsky and to his music. We might assert in general that even resorting to the alibi of delegating certain elements of the composition process to "objective" factors always has a subjective

---

92   KUNDERA, Milan. *O hudbě a románu*. Brno: Atlantis, 2014, p. 24.

93   ZAGORSKI, Marcus. *Kapitoly z estetiky seriálnej hudby*. Transl. by Robert Kolář. Edice Paralely. Bratislava: Asociácia Corpus a NM Code, 2017.

94   DAHLHAUS, Carl. A Rejection of Material Thinking? In *Schoenberg and the New Music*. Translated by Derrick Puffet and Alfred Clayton. Cambridge, 1987, p. 276, quoted in ZAGORSKI, op. cit., 2017.

cause because every resignation of authorship is the author's purely subjective and individual decision. Nonetheless, it must be said that music has historically always contained certain objective components, such as traces of period style, compositional technique, rhetoric, and paradigms that accelerated or simplified a work, made it accessible, or fixed it historically and geographically. It was technology that played the main role in this process as a mechanical, formalising, and algorithmizing principle.

3.3 Technological transformations of the parameters of modern music

Until the beginning of the 20th century, music and musicology as theoretical reflection on music were working mainly with the tone as material (thence the German term 'Tonkunst'). Developmentally, this is given by the fact that European musical traditions are based on monophonic singing, which was later replaced by a musical instrument. For multiple voices in parallel, rules were established from acoustics based on the physical nature of vibrating objects. From that, the entire harmonic system of music from the 16th through the 21st centuries was derived. The microintervals typical of Arabic or Indian (Indonesian) cultures never caught on for very long in European music although they can easily be derived from the higher tones of the harmonic series.

The existence of musical tradition depends upon memory, in which it is stored in a fixed form. Developmentally, the oldest kind of storage medium is human memory, which is bound to the organ that most closely reproduces its content, the human voice. What cannot be reproduced by the human voice can only become the content of human memory with difficulty. Of course, we cannot forget the connection to the word. The melody of speech seems to be the reason why European folk music is mostly based on tones.

From units that are sufficiently identifiable by their frequencies and can be fixed in the memory, i.e. tones, we arrive at the highest level of creative thinking for this type of material, namely the art of music.

At the beginning of the 20th century, music was the most highly developed and most comprehensive artificially created system for the arrangement of sensory elements in time and space. This is a dynamic system in several dimensions that is often composed of dozens of layers (like in a Mahler symphony), which are acoustically and temporally coordinated. This sophisticated system of spatiotemporal relationships becomes the departure point for other media such as film (or for video games or digital games later on).

We must necessarily ask how the basic elements of music have reacted to the technological innovations of the 20th and 21st centuries. If we take as our departure point the basic music theory of the 20th century, we come up with the following musical elements: kinetics (movement), melody, harmony (chords), dynamics, colour (timbre), structure/tectonics (formal structure), and spatial relationships.

Until the beginning of the 20th century, three basic parameters of musical organisation were predominant: pitch (frequency), length (duration), and volume (dynamics), and a fourth (timbre) gradually awakened after the arrival of musical Impressionism. The 1930s saw the emergence of practical and theoretical attempts to add space as a fifth parameter of sound/music. The author of this book has already devoted himself to this matter in some earlier studies,[95] so it will receive only limited space here. In relation to music or sound in space, one must mention at least the following paradigmatic nodal points: in the lecture *The Liberation of Sound* delivered by Edgard Varèse in Santa Fe (USA) in 1936, he codifies a fourth dimension of music—besides the horizontal, vertical, and dynamic (he does not mention timber), he discusses the projection of sound in space.[96] At the time, he was considering the realisation of the global utopian project *Espace* (1929-), which was to have used radio to connect musical performances in metropolises around the world into a single whole. Another important technologically constructed sonic reality was his *Poème électronique* (1958), in which Varèse realised his lifelong vision of sound as an object that can be manipulated in space.[97]

Since the 1920s, radio has been a key technology becoming a medium of the colonisation of space by sound. Artists who are drawn to radio mostly see speed and audience size as its most attractive aspects. The radio receiver is gradually becoming a more-or-less predictable musical instrument (John Cage: *Imaginary Landscape No. 4*) and a home for unexpected audio collages and montages. Radio has also brought new artistic genres like radio opera. Pioneering examples include the "radio cantata" *Der Lindberghflug* (1929) by Paul Hindemith, Bertolt Brecht, and Kurt Weill or Bohuslav Martinů's radio operas *Hlas lesa* (The Voice of the Forest), H. 243 and *Veselohra na mostě* (Comedy on the Bridge), H. 247 (both from 1935). Other areas of artistic creation came into existence in radio studios (first RTF in Paris and WDR in Germany), where various schools of electronic music emerged after the Second World War.

In Germany, Karlheinz Stockhausen followed Varèse chronologically in his Darmstadt lecture *Musik im Raum* (1958). At the time, he was also doing practical experiments with the spatial diffusion of sound. Putting aside his spatial compositions with purely acoustical instrumentation like *Gruppen* and *Carré*, and mention must at least be made of *Gesang der Jünglinge* and *Kontakte* with multichannel sound distribution.[98] John Cage had a completely different way of working with sound in space. In his multimedia work *Variations V* (1965), he used the movement of dancers

---

95   FLAŠAR, Martin. *Karlheinz Stockhausen: hudba a prostor*. Bachelor's thesis. Supervisor: Prof. PhDr. Miloš Štědroň, CSc. Masarykova univerzita, 2003; FLAŠAR, Martin. *Poème électronique, 1958: Le Corbusier, E. Varèse, I. Xenakis*. Brno: Masarykova univerzita, 2012. Spisy Masarykovy univerzity v Brně, Filozofická fakulta.

96   VARÈSE, Edgard. *Die Befreiung des Klangs*. Übersetzt von R. Riehn. In CHARBONNIER, Georges. *Entretiens avec Edgard Varèse*. Paris: Belfond, 1970, p. 12.

97   FLAŠAR, Martin. *Poème électronique*, op. cit., 2012

98   FLAŠAR, Martin. *Karlheinz Stockhausen*, op. cit., 2003.

in space as an interactive controller of an audio-visual system with audio and video projections.

The arrival of electronic technologies in the 20th century mainly impacted the musical parameters of colour (timbre) and space. While until the 20th century, timbre (i.e. the spectral characteristic of sound) remained exclusively dependent upon the chosen combinations of musical instruments, their registers, and various playing techniques, in the 20th century there took place a colonisation of music by electronic technologies (electroacoustic music), which enabled musicians including composers and performers to manipulate sounds that cannot be produced with traditional instruments. The possibilities of artificially synthesised sound introduced virtual instruments that had never been heard before or combinations of instruments or sounds that had not previously been realised. A very specific area is the overlap between acoustical and electroacoustic music on the basis of timbre. Already in the 1950s we find uncertainty among various composers of New Music in their choice of resources for timbre-based music. Some dealt with the problem on a purely acoustical level (e.g. I. Xenakis in *Metastaseis*), some gave preference to electroacoustics (P. Henry, K. Stockhausen), some sought a synthesis of both areas (E. Varèse: *Déserts*), and still others, having had experience with electroacoustic music, gave up using its resources and achieved the same results using purely acoustical methods (G. Ligeti).

Filip Johánek recently devoted himself to the kinetic aspect of 20th-century music in connection with technology in his study *Vztah technologie a rytmu v hudbě 20. a 21. století* (The Relationship between Technology and Rhythm in the Music of the 20th and 21st Centuries).[99] In it he mainly follows the transformation taking place in musical thinking under the influence first of mechanical, then later of electronic technologies.

> "[…] the regular and periodic sound of machines seeped into the audio culture of the Machine Age, and this was reflected by musical creators who then distributed it further into space when they created compositions with regular rhythms. Compositions with regular rhythms then in turn influenced audio culture and especially listeners and other composers."[100]

While Johánek attempts to show how the regular rhythm of the mechanical era left its mark on music of the period (which is difficult to prove because regular rhythm is already characteristic of music of the preindustrial era), with the electronic technologies characteristic of the post-industrial area, he himself says it is not possible to prove that the irregularity of sonic events connected with this technology leads to their application in music. He merely asserts (and one really must agree with this conclusion) that the post-industrial era has produced

---

99   JOHÁNEK, Filip. *Vztah technologie a rytmu v hudbě 20. a 21. století.* Master's thesis. Supervisor: PhDr. Martin Flašar, Ph.D. Brno: Masarykova Univerzita, 2014.

100   Ibid., p. 50.

technological instruments that have made it possible to set in stone and work with irregularities in music.[101]

Early in the 20th century, noise (or non-musical sound) seemed to be a medium with lesser expressive potential than tones. It soon turned out, however, that this was probably because of the limited capability to manipulate non-musical sound. Instruments that use unpitched sound are mostly percussion, and in view of the instruments' physical design, it is difficult to achieve a higher variability of sound output from them. The situation changes the moment when the physical instrument and the sound are dislocated[102] (or disassociated). As soon as sound becomes a sound object and abandons its physical carrier, its sounding medium,[103] it becomes a freely transformable virtual object. At the same time, it must be fixed in a new kind of recording medium (such as a recording cylinder, LP record, film strip, magnetic tape etc.).

The new type of manipulation of a sound object that Pierre Schaeffer came up with after the Second World War at RTF was initially still the manipulation of physical media (closed groove method, cutting and splicing magnetic tape etc.) for the purpose of manipulating their audio content, but with the arrival of digital technologies (perhaps for the first time in 1957 in the *ILLIAC Suite for String Quartet*), the manipulation of sound ceases to be a physical matter and becomes an abstract, algorithmic-mathematical operation.

Of course, with respect to art theory, we remain in the realm of music. We are discussing *musique concrète*, acousmatic music, *Elektronische Musik*, electroacoustic music etc., but sound as an abstract object has now set out on its own independent path through history. A real change of paradigm would mean defining sound art as a category. The first use of the term is disputed, but it was apparently in 1974 on the cover of the Something Else Yearbook.[104] As Alan Licht[105] points out, that designation overlaps with other categories like new music, experimental music, noise, sampling etc. In German, the term Klangkunst is used in parallel.

In musicological discourse, the term "sound art" sounds somewhat out of place because it is understood as an artistic movement or a set of strategies that is more of an outgrowth of the visual arts than of music. This can be best explained in terms of the intermedia concept of the 1960s, when one might find visual artists with an orientation towards expression in the field of sound and musicians striving for the materialisation or objectivization of their sound works in the same place. More enlightened artists and theorists are trying to incorporate the new term into the field of music (e.g. Edgard Varèse, John Cage, Leigh Landy etc.) by redefining what the word "music" means.

---

101   Ibid.

102   Cf. RATAJ, Michal. O zvuku, který se hýbe v nás i kolem nás. In RATAJ, Michal et al. *Zvukoprostor - prostorozvuk*. Praha: NAMU, 2018. Chapter 5. *Dislokace - prostorové oddělení*.

103   Cf. FUKAČ, Jiří. *Pojmosloví hudební komunikace*. Brno: Masarykova univerzita, 1991, p. 40.

104   GÁL, Bernhard. Updating the History of Sound Art: Additions, Clarifications, More Questions. *Leonardo Music Journal*. 2017, 27, p. 79.

105   LICHT, Alan. *Sound Art: Beyond Music, Between Categories*. New York: Rizzoli, 2007, pp. 11–12.

What was characteristic of the situation of modern music, which slowly dissolved in the 1970s, was a striving for novelty and originality. This was the source of the prideful designation New Music (die Neue Musik), which was in use in Germany and later in Europe more broadly in the 20th century. The contemporary German philosopher Peter Sloterdijk characteristically defined modernity as a "culture of fast ignition" or even an explosion of surplus energy.[106] It is therefore no wonder that a sign of modern culture is the mechanical device, which becomes equally an instrument of creativity and a target of criticism.

The era of electricity-powered mechanical devices gave rise to electroacoustic music, which became the most suitable tool for exploring and composing sound. This amounts to a remarkable tautology: sound is explored using the tools that originally gave birth to it as a byproduct of the industrial revolution.

In the transition from modernist to the postmodernist thinking, we have tried to identify three types of creative attitudes towards technology: techno-utopian/ techno-optimistic, techno-realistic, and techno-sceptic/post-technological. One cannot simply assert that the chronological transition between individual stages is developmentally conditioned, no matter how tempting that idea might appear to be. Already during the initial, enthusiastic discovery of technologies in the first half of the 20th century, voices critical of technology could be heard, just as deep into the postmodern era we find authors who believe in the innovative potential of technologically conditioned music.

3.4 Technologies of Altermodernism: more modern than Postmodernism

Since the 1950s, modern mechanical devices have successively been replaced by electronic tools and eventually by the digital computers of the post-industrial era. The material, analogue traces of sound are dissolved into binary code, which is inert, homogenous, and entirely isolated from the original sound medium. Binary code is the ideal medium for the articulation of plurality, which rather soon came to be called the Postmodern, especially by J.-F. Lyotard. Binary code definitively destroys the idea of solid media (as tangible machines) and enables free transitions each time between newly constructed forms of expression. Depending upon the user's interactive needs, is possible to interpret at any time as an image, sound, video, virtual space etc. Just like remediation (M. McLuhan, J. D. Bolter, and R. A. Grusin) of older forms of media in a software environment, it removes the barriers between the arts, and the convergence of these forms (H. Jenkins) brings the possibility of their accumulation in one spatiotemporal framework and gives rise to multimedia that are retroactively

---

106　SLOTERDIJK, Peter. La pensée sphérique. *BAM*, 2004, No. 2, Vies modes d'emploi, p. 192. Quoted in BOURRIAUD, Nicolas. *Altermodern*. In *Altermodern: Tate Triennial 2009*. London: Tate Publishing, 2009.

applied like a metaphorical concept for the "reading" of older symbolic "texts" as in, for example, Richard Wagner's Gesamtkunstwerk or a sound film.[107]

Postmodernism appears on the European intellectual scene in ca. 1973 as a tendency to revise modern development. Bourriaud[108] compares it to depression from the loss of progress of technical and cultural ideologies, and he recalls the end of the understanding of history as developing linearly and, in agreement with Lyotard, the collapse of their "grand narratives".

> "Postmodernism is a philosophy of grieving, a long, melancholy episode in our cultural life. When history lost its direction and the ability to read, there was nothing left to do but stand face to face with immobilised spacetime, in which mutilated fragments of the past arose as reminiscences [...]."[109]

It is worth commenting here that the loss of faith in technological progress is not the same thing as the actual absence of development. Although postmodernism can be regarded as an expression of critical societal attitudes towards innovations and their function, technological development has continued without interruption in the fields of audio technology and electroacoustic music. For example, a paradoxical tension has arisen between the return of the aesthetics of old music since 1970 and the development of new sound technologies, digital instruments, software, communications interfaces etc.

In 2009 Bourriaud proposed the new term "Altermodernism". Although he comments that Altermodernism is mainly characterised by its timelessness and universality, one might boldly oppose him by asserting that Altermodernism is, to the contrary, very closely tied to the time of its emergence. While we understand Postmodernism as a reaction to modernity, and its existence is justified mainly as the antithesis of the modern, Altermodernism seems to be just another of the terms derived from the word "modern". This is also the real intent of the author: he is trying to recapture the basic gesture of modernism, which is, according to him, escape, exodus, setting out on a journey, nomadism. Of course, this is a partially problematic assertion. Certainly one cannot call into question the basic departure points of Modernism, which include rebellion against tradition. (This is something we also find in the name of the Vienna Secession as well as in the text of the Czech manifesto of Literary Modernism.) Nonetheless, in his typology of postmodern man, Zygmunt Bauman also included nomadism among the characteristic features of Postmodernism.[110] Within that term, we differentiate between idlers, wanderers,

---

107   Cf. PACKER, Randall and JORDAN, Ken. *Multimedia: From Wagner to Virtual Reality*. New York: W. W. Norton, c2002.

108   BOURRIAUD, Nicolas, op. cit.

109   Ibid.

110   BAUMAN, Zygmunt. *Úvahy o postmoderní době* [Dva szkice o moralności ponowoczesnej; Ciało i przemoc w obliczu ponowoczesności]. Praha: Sociologické nakladatelství, 2002. For expanded critical discussion, cf. VERMEULEN, Timotheus and AKKER, Robin van den. Notes on Metamodernism. *Journal of Aesthetics & Culture*, 2: 1, 5677, 2010.

tourists, and players. In fact, the metaphor of the wanderer personality type overlaps almost identically with Bourriaud's definition of a nomad (*homo viator*). What, then, is the difference between Altermodernism and Postmodernism if both work with the concept of the nomad?

The word "Altermodernism", which is meant to refer to the void after postmodernity, is etymologically derived from the Latin word *"alter"* = "different". It should evoke diversity and differentness, in short, an alternative to the one path. It is a synthesis of the principles of modernity and the global present day. It is intended to be an escape from nationalism, reification of thinking and practice, and consumerist unification. Bourriaud imagines it as a heterochronous (temporally pluralistic), heterotopical (global), and heterosemiotic (intertextual) discourse, in which contemporary artists head out on their own paths into the spatiotemporal universe of signs in order to blaze the trail for new forms of artworks on their own original trajectories.

Whatever Bourriaud's intention may have been (overlooking promotion of his exhibition with the same title at London's Tate Modern), the whole essay exudes the spirit of revolt against stale Postmodernism. One cannot help the impression that this is a case of wishful thinking. Bourriaud's arguments for new paradigms are not very convincing. In other words, there is very little reason to believe that what we are talking about is anything other than Postmodernism seen differently. Some theoreticians actually see Postmodernism as the continuation of Modernism by different means. Just as problematic to a considerable degree is the competing term "Neo-Postmodernism", which has been calling for the return of modern features to the arts since the end of the 20th century. We will probably have to wait a bit longer for the outcome of this confusing dispute over terminology. What is certain is that there are voices calling for change, just as it is certain that change must come.

Linda Ioanna Kouvaras[111] sees the renaissance of acousmatic music as an example of the new modernity in contemporary sound creation. The acousmonium created by François Bayle in Paris in 1974 was not the swansong of French electroacoustic music, but instead a rather surprising springboard into the 21st century. However much an orchestra consisting of speakers might strike us as the result of the futuristic enchantment of fading Modernism, in recent decades we see a lively interest at European universities in similar equipment for the spatial projection of sound (SARC at Queens University in Belfast, BEAST at the University of Birmingham, the MTIRC acousmonium at De Montfort University in Leicester, the acousmonium at the Academy of Performing Arts in Prague etc.).

The current resurfacing of spatial music and of the acousmonium as the supreme apparatus of the analogue electroacoustic era indicates that in the development of art music and sound art, we are becoming weary of digitality and computer music. It is not that composers are ridding themselves of multimedia computers, but rather that computer music is ceasing to be an exciting topic.

---

111   KOUVARAS, Linda Ioanna. *Loading the Silence: Australian Sound Art in the Post-Digital Age.* Routledge, 2013.

Were we to highlight the greatest discovery of 20ᵗʰ-century music, it would be sound in all its forms—sound as a material for creative thinking and for structuring in space-time. All electronic technologies are just tools for manipulating sound. If we were now to rid ourselves of them, sound is all that would remain—sound that can just as well be made by banging two rocks together as by direct digital synthesis in a computer. The problem, the development of which we can follow over the last 100 years, is how musicology as a traditional field deals with sound material. The first possibility is that traditional musicology attempts to absorb sound art. The second possibility is the emergence of a far broader field of sonology, which will engulf historical musicology because of the obvious disparity between the two fields. The third and clearly most probable possibility is that musicology will continue to exist alongside studies of audio culture and sound art as a minority field specialising in the small, exclusive segment of sound art that we call music.

Chapter 4

The Musical Work in the Process of Abstraction, Digitisation, and Materialisation

> "Finally, this relation can be expressed in a mathematical form, as the irregular rather than the regular figures seem to count. The figurative remains as the final abstract expression in any art."[112]
>
> Wassily Kandinsky

4.1 From abstraction to digitisation

In the course of the 20th century, two lines of development converge: the line of the arts leading to abstraction and the line of technological development leading from the mechanical (industrial) era to the information (post-industrial) era. If we begin by focusing on the first line, we encounter several paradoxes. If we discuss abstraction in music, after all, we risk using a tautological argument: music is one of the most abstract artforms by its very nature, provided that we understand abstraction as the absence of subjectivity on the level of function or content. The material of music is intangible (consisting only of vibrations spreading in a particular environment), and its manipulation takes place indirectly at a symbolic level (musical notation) or by the handling of physical instruments that produce or reproduce soundwaves. In the 1920s, there came about the replacement of traditional musical notation symbolising the parameters of tone (or sound) like duration, pitch, timbre, and volume with numerical values and series of numbers. Music is thus literally digitalised, meaning that it is represented numerically. Numerical representation is a condition for and enables a number of other processes described by new media theorists, such as formalizability, algorithmisation, compressibility, automatisation, modularity, hypertextuality, networkability, interactivity etc.[113]

---

112   KANDINSKY, Wassily. *On the Spiritual in Art*. Hilla Rebay (ed.). New York: Guggenheim Foundation, 1946, p. 90.

113   Cf. e.g. MANOVICH, Lev. *The Language of New Media*. Cambridge, Mass.: MIT Press, 2000; LISTER, Martin. *New media: A Critical Introduction*. 2nd ed. Milton Park, Abingdon, Oxon: Routledge, 2009 or FELDMAN, Tony. *An Introduction to Digital Media*. New York: Routledge, 2003.

The rationalisation of music reached unprecedented depths in the first half of the 20th century. Arnold Schoenberg's dodecaphony and postwar serialism introduced mathematical methods to music as an expression of growing abstraction in the arts. Mathematical conceptions of music are not an "invention" of the 20th century, but rather a great return, as Friedrich Herzfeld points out: *"The fact that we deal with so many numbers in music is perhaps not proof of the modern hegemony of technology, [...], instead it means a return to the law of world order [...]".*[114] Homogenous numerical code is becoming the common denominator for all kinds of art. This fact was already noticed by a member of the group Der blaue Reiter, Wassily Kandinsky, when he commented that in every artform, the number remains the most remote expression. One of the great overall mathematical conceptions of music is the treatise *Formalized Music* by the Greek-French composer and architect, Iannis Xenakis (1922–2001).[115]

"In 1954, I introduced probability theory and calculus in musical composition in order to control sound masses both in their invention and in their evolution. This inaugurated an entirely new path in music, more global than polyphony, serialism or, in general, 'discrete' music", wrote Xenakis.[116] The new path he is talking about is stochastic music, i.e. music based on the theory of probability. By its application, Xenakis was reacting to discoveries in the realms of statistical physics and information theory, and specifically the concept of entropy as understood by Ludwig Boltzmann and Claude E. Shannon. Stochastic music is based on the aesthetic perception of concrete manifestations of mathematical relationships. Xenakis discusses "stochastic dynamics" that are "aesthetically interesting", and he also puts music at the level of science:

> "[...] the flux of time is locally equipped with a structure of total order in a mathematical sense. That is to say that its image in our brain, an image constituted by the chain of successive events, can be placed in one-to-one correspondance [sic!] with the integers and even, with the aid of a useful generalization, with real numbers (rational and irrational). Thus, it can be counted. This is what the sciences in general do, and music as well, by using its own clock, the metronome. By virtue of this same structure of total order, time can be placed in a one-to-one correspondence with the points of a line. It can thus be drawn. This is done in the sciences, but also in music."[117]

François Delalande also emphasises the storage function of recording apart from the actual time of composition in his book *Le son des musiques: Entre technologie et estétique.*[118] In it, he divides music history into three basic paradigms:

---

114   HERZFELD, Friedrich. *Musica nova.* Praha: Mladá fronta, 1966. Kolumbus, p. 173.

115   XENAKIS, Iannis. *Formalized Music: Thought and Mathematics in Composition.* Additional material compiled and edited by Sharon Kanach. Stuyvesant, N.Y.: Pendragon Press, 1992.

116   Ibid., p. 255.

117   Ibid., p. 264.

118   DELALANDE, François. *Le son des musiques: Entre technologie et esthétique.* Paris: INA/GRM Buchet/ Chastel, 2001. Quoted in LANDY, Leigh. *Understanding the Art of Sound Organization.* Cambridge, Mass.: MIT Press, c2007, p. 178.

1. oral tradition,
2. the tradition of musical notation (music put in fixed form by notation),
3. electroacoustic paradigms (music recorded on a physical medium).

Delalande's perspective in this categorisation gives priority to the technological criterion of the creating of fixed content of a musical work without considering the nature of the sound material, as Leigh Landy proposes.[119] There are further implications to be drawn from this observation. A categorisation based on storage media implies ways of manipulating music. For example, in the oral tradition, apart from reproduction, only basic ways of manipulating music that is fixed in human memory can be used, such as improvisation and ornamentation. In the tradition of musical notation, it becomes possible to create complex intellectual constructions, and electroacoustic technologies make it possible not only to work directly with the sound itself, but also to break it down analytically into its basic elements and to manipulate its structure. It is mainly reproduction that is within the possibilities of the oral tradition, musical notation enables composition with whole musical units, and electroacoustic technologies grant entry into the sound itself, with which one can work directly at its "microscopic" level. The level of intellectual complexity of musical operations is thus strictly dependent upon the music's storage medium.

The practice of electroacoustic music of the 20th century drew attention to a number of important features that had been previously underappreciated. This mainly involves the key role of:

1. the performer and live performance,
2. the presence of an instrument enabling live action,
3. the uniform spatiotemporal framework of production and reception.

This component of musical communication was influenced, disrupted, or redefined by the arrival of technological music.

4.2 Dead music and the absence of a performer

The practice of purely acousmatic music (*rien à voir*) introduced at the turn of the 1940s and '50s by Pierre Schaeffer in France and a few years later by Karlheinz Stockhausen in Germany satisfied the demand for concentrated listening undisturbed by visual sensations, but at the same time it affirmed the deeply ingrained causal connection between a visible action and sound or between sight and hearing. An audible sensation is always perceived as the result or sign of a physical action. Of course, the dissociation of cause and effect or of the sign and of what is signified had already appeared developmentally in music. Examples include instruments playing offstage, liturgical music, musical recordings, sound film,

---

119 LANDY, Leigh, op. cit., c2007, p. 178.

radio broadcasts etc. There were two separate causes for the dissociation of human action and music: either the kind of music involved had a heteronomous function that would by disturbed by the presence of the performer in the field of vision, or the dissociation was the result of the inadequacy of the technology. This means that if the possibility of making audio-visual recordings had been available in the 19th century, we certainly would have used it instead of making purely audio recordings. The new thing in this scheme is the production of artificial music that is artistically autonomous without the presence of visually perceptible action. Again, this was the result of technological necessity because the manipulation of electroacoustic music was, with some exceptions, impossible in the 1950s. However, this situation exposed the weaknesses of musical communication in which the performer appears as a basic assumption of the audience, thereby drawing attention to the performative, theatrical character of live music. If public radio broadcast listening sessions were regarded as a societal sensation at the beginning of the 1920s due to the very lack of diegetic perception, the same practice in acousmatic music, repeated over time, affirmed the need for and importance of the performer as the originator of musical sound. Those listening to acousmatic music are denied participation in the causality of the creation of music in real time, and that is clearly the greatest adventure and value of music that is produced live. The listener of acousmatic music knows nothing about the music's origin, has no idea whether it is the outcome of complex or simple processes, and lacks any scale of reference for the human effort that must be exerted for the creation of such music.

The importance of the distinction between authentic and mediated experience is firmly established in our languages. We say "live music" to refer to an authentic musical experience, but we do not use the readily available term "dead music" for the form of musical experience that is determined *a priori* by notation or *a posteriori*[120] by recording, but instead we call such music "notated" or "recorded". Nonetheless, these two forms are fundamentally different. *A priori* determination embodies the potential for audible music that is to be actualised and performed by an interpreter in the context of a live, shared cultural experience. *A posteriori* determination is a truly dead imprint of music, which is a recording of just one of the infinite set of realisations within the framework of the act of interpretation. The definitive and "dead" character of this music can be partially overcome by the recipient only by an active approach to the dramaturgical selection of various interpretations of the same composition. The ambiguousness of interpretation can then hint at the set of forms a single work can assume, but it is not capable of changing the isolated conditions of listening.

---

120   BOSSIS, Bruno. The Analysis of Electroacoustic Music: from Sources to Invariants. *Organised Sound*, 2006, 11, No. 2, pp. 101–112.

4.3 Fragmentation of the production-reception spatiotemporal framework

Until the emergence of the first technologies for recording music such as the phonograph (1877) and the gramophone record (1887), the making of musical sound and its reception were as a rule subject to a unitary spatiotemporal framework, which brought performers and listeners together and created a foundation for shared culture. Listeners who wanted to hear music had to find themselves in the same place and at the same time as the player of a musical instrument or the singer. With the arrival of technologies enabling the recording and subsequent reproduction of sound, the authenticity of sounding music was cancelled. Walter Benjamin dealt with this phenomenon sufficiently in the essay *The Work of Art in the Age of Mechanical Reproduction* (*Das Kunstwerk im Zeitalter seiner technischen Reproduzierbarkeit*, 1936), in which for the authenticity and genuineness of a work of art he used the word "aura", which is constructed by the existence of a work of art in time and space, and which takes part in shaping its uniqueness. By mechanical copying, this uniqueness is lost for the sake of mass-scale availability. Under the influence of recording and copying technology, the Shannon-Weaver linear communication model of transmitter-channel-receiver in time and space is becoming fragmented. Sound has been separated from the action that produced it and ripped out of its original spatiotemporal context, enabling its further use in new contexts as a sound object. Rid of the action that created it, sound becomes a semantic sign or gesture without a cause, a non-sensual object that reacquires meaning by insertion into a new rational structure. The phonograph, the gramophone record, the magnetic tape, the CD and DVD, and new media enabling the storing of a growing volume of initially continuous (analog) then later discrete encoded (digital) musical information in a smaller and smaller physical space have led to the literal "disappearance" of music.

We call this process the compression of musical information. Of course, the principle of compression was already contained in the very foundations of musical notation. As an example, there are the graphic symbols for the semibreve / breve / longa / maxima or later the sixteenth / eighth / quarter / half / whole note, with a single symbol of constant size to indicate various durations. In general, the condition of compression can be said to be the very principle of the symbolic representation of music or of the translation of music from the aural to the visual sphere, or in other words, the translating of music from time into space.

The goal of musical thinking and creativity is sounding work because it is only in that form that the music (or its author) can communicate with listeners. On the basis of that logic, it might seem more suitable to preserve recordings of Mahler's symphonies than their scores, but the problem is that if we were to get rid of the scores, we would lose the possibility of the future study, performing, and recording of the compositions. We might give as an example the tragedies and comedies of Shakespeare. Digital audiovisual recordings have now been made of them, but we do not burn the texts and scripts because of that. What is involved here is not just the existence of a work realised in a culture, but also the possibility of realising or reconstructing it at any time. In this way, culture actually affirms the importance of the repeated interpretation of works of art. The reason for this is either fear of the impossibility of actualisation, or—and this is more likely—the desire to be repeatedly present at the act of the unique reconstitution of a work under new conditions. This is a creative game that is played under changing temporal, spatial, societal, political, and other conditions on the basis of the unchanging script or score, employing a powerful aesthetic combination of the old and new, the familiar and the surprising. In the 20th century, J. Huizinga and H.-G. Gadamer thoroughly discussed the relationship between culture and playing.[121] The compression of music has far-reaching consequences that we will probably not be able to investigate here in all of its particulars. Clearly, in musical operations, compression is connected with the saving of space for the storage of information and the dissemination of music.

Mark Katz investigates the relationship between live and reproduced music in the plentifully quoted publication *Capturing Sound: How Technology has Changed Music.*[122] In chapter 1 he proposes a set of distinctive features of musical recordings. Some of them, however, can be successfully disputed:

1. **Tangibility** – Katz asserts that unlike music that is performed live, a musical recording as an object has a physical nature (LP record, cassette tape, CD, DVD etc.). Such a claim is problematical, however, because it applies to the physical recording medium and not to the recording itself. By analogy, we might claim that live music is dependent on the physical musical instruments.
2. **Portability** – the portability of recordings enables the exchange of music across cultures, space, and time, and in connection with certain genres, the author even speaks of there being "record cultures" (reggae, hip-hop etc.).
3. **(In)visibility** – music is socially and culturally communicable thanks to its visibility. Music performed live is a multimodal experience involving both vision and hearing. Music has often been invisible in connection with spiritual experiences (sacred music performed in the church's choir loft, initiation rituals of non-European cultures etc.). The invisibility of the source also accentuates the exclusively auditory aspect of music.
4. **Repeatability** – live music is unrepeatable. The repeatability of listening to a recording leads to the diverting of attention towards the interpretation. Repetition becomes a compositional principle (most visibly, for example, in *minimal music*), and the composers and musicians become listeners.
5. **Temporality** – the length of compositions and their selection are limited by the capacity of recording media (playing length of LP records, data volume of

---

121 HUIZINGA, Johan. *Homo Ludens: A Study of the Play-Element in Culture.* Boston: Beacon, c1955.; GADAMER, Hans-Georg. *The Relevance of the Beautiful and Other Essays.* Cambridge University Press, 1986.

122 KATZ, Mark. *Capturing Sound: How Technology Has Changed Music.* Rev. ed. Berkeley: University of California Press, c2010.

CDs, DVDs etc.). We might add that the limitation of quantity or length caused by media capacity has been overcome by streaming (radio, television, online streaming services), which can offer a basically endless flow of music.

6. **Receptivity** – the listening conditions are retroactively inserted into recordings, which are supplied with artificial reverb, echoes, spatial placement (panning) etc. For example, the entire genre of electroacoustic music bears the characteristic of receptivity, with the listening experience already contained in the musical work itself.

4.4 Music as the subject and object of media

Dematerialisation or disembodiment as a process characteristic of the arts in the era of the new media are not appropriate designations in the case of music because music has never consisted of physical material. It has always been not only the subject, but also the object of other media that provide for music's production, transmission, and recording. As a subject, music has communicated content that it was capable of mediating as a system of symbols. Such content has been encoded in music either deliberately during its creation or has been foisted on the music (by force to a greater or lesser degree) during the act of interpretation.

Music finds itself in the function of an object in relation to the following media:

1. **Sound-producing media.** In the case of music, there has always been compensation for the absence of physical material by the presence of a definite sound-producing medium that directly determined the nature of the music being produced. In older music, this was musical instruments, then from the 20th century there have been electronic technologies that guarantee the resulting form of the sound.[123]

2. **Distribution media.** For a very long time, the premises of churches, (concert) halls, "other spaces" (*espaces autres* in the sense of Foucault's heterotopias[124]) etc. served as the distribution media of music. This formerly firmly determined space with clearly given characteristics has become a variable, fluid medium, which imprints its own characteristic features onto the original "text". The new distribution channels for music (like radio, television, recordings on physical media, or the internet) have partially replaced direct means of sharing the consumption of music, as has been described above.

3. **Recording media.** There is probably no need here for deeper analysis of recording media. Basically, it can be said with some simplification that the media follow the advancements of technology. This development leads to transformation of the

---

123 Cf. FUKAČ, Jiří, op. cit., 1991. Chapter 1.7.3 *Média rozeznění.*

124 FOUCAULT, Michel. *Of Other Spaces: Utopias and Heterotopias* [online]. [Des Espace Autres, March 1967], in *Architecture /Mouvement/ Continuité* in October, 1984. Translated from the French by Jay Miskowiec. [Accessed on 22 Oct. 2018]. Retrieved from: http://web.mit.edu/allanmc/www/foucault1.pdf.

encoding of musical notation or recordings. The ability to decode the code in question is the prerequisite for the survival of music of entire historical epochs or of shorter periods. This applies both to reading the musical notation of the *ars nova* period and to understanding the MP3 lossy compression algorithm. Besides preserving music in the relevant code, one must also preserve the technology and its description to be able to reconstruct the music.

The major breakthrough in the development of the encoding of music was digitisation, i.e. transformation into the form of a numerical code (usually binary or hexadecimal). Digitisation has "dissolved" works of all kinds into homogenous code that can be interpreted in reverse within the context of any artistic genre. This makes the code easy to transfer from one artistic genre to another. There is no reason why a digitised picture might not be heard as an audio work, or motion might not direct light projection etc.

4. **Media reflections on music.** We can regard media reflections and meta-reflections on music as being the most remote from the original "text". In this category, we could include a concert programme, a newspaper review, a television programme, discussions among academicians and laypersons etc. To a certain degree, their function is informational or reconstructive (through them, the original "text" can be brought to life).

4.5 (Re)construction of digital music

The digitisation of sound, i.e. its numerical representation, has moved the whole question of abstraction in music one level deeper. Were we to attempt to express the relationship between sounding music and its representation on a scale of degrees, in the case of the paradigm of musical notation[125] we would get the following categories:

1. sounding music,
2. performance,
3. musical notation,
4. numerical representation of music.

Here, the digital form of music is the numerical representation of notation, i.e. the meta-representation of sounding music. In this case, however, this involves digital representation within the context of an older paradigm.

In the newer (electroacoustical) paradigm, the hierarchy of relationships is as follows:

1. sounding music,
2. reproduction / reconstruction,
3. numerical representation of music,
(4. compression).

---

125   DELALANDE, op. cit.

While reproduction is a widely comprehensible term used in connection with playback of music in the context of recording technologies, reconstruction is a term proposed by Martin Knakkergaard. In his study *Unsound Sound: On the Ontology of Sound in the Digital Age*,[126] he makes the logical argument that digital information in the form of code is intangible, so one cannot properly speak of the reproduction, but rather of the construction or reconstruction of music. We should add that this is the fundamental distinction between analogue and digital audio information. There is a huge difference between playing back a recording from an LP record and the reconstruction of recorded sound on the basis of digital code, e.g. from a CD or streaming.

> "[...] the digital can be read at will because sound and music are no longer reproduced but reconstructed. Or constructed. For we can read binary tables as 'anything', without regard to how and by what they are formed."[127]

In his groundbreaking book *The Language of New Media*,[128] Lev Manovich discusses the double representation that is characteristic of new media. For the purposes of musical thinking in the context of new media, we could transform it into the following form:

MUSICAL THINKING

MUSICAL NOTATION

(representation of the 1st order; symbolic representation)

DIGITAL CODE

(representation of the 2nd order; numerical meta-representation)

Knakkergaard goes on to inquire into the actual nature of this "new materiality" of music. He notices the major changes to the process of composing in the digital media environment, where not only sound, but also musical instruments are dematerialised. A DAW (Digital Audio Workstation) is a virtual studio in which audio information is just as non-real as all the instruments that the creators have at their disposal. At the same time, it represents a combination of all the previously separate forms of music's existence: concrete forms of sounding music and their abstract representation.

Knakkergaard employs the device of Aristotelean causality to describe the entire schema.[129] However useful this method may be, the author's examples assigned to individual causes are not acceptable without reservations or can be the subject of

---

126 KNAKKERGAARD, Martin. Unsound Sound: On the Ontology of Sound in the Digital Age. *Leonardo Music Journal*, 2016, Vol. 26, pp. 64–67.

127 Ibid., p. 64.

128 MANOVICH, Lev. *The Language of New Media*. Cambridge, Mass.: MIT Press, 2000.

129 KNAKKERGAARD, op. cit., p. 65.

debate. For example, he classifies musical instruments among the formal causes, but it would seem more appropriate to place them among the efficient causes. Likewise, one cannot agree with classifying tones among the formal causes, as they rather belong among the material causes. It is also unclear why he classifies style among the formal causes and genre among the final causes. We would propose the following revision:

1. causa materialis – sounds, tones, noises, hiss;
2. causa formalis – forms, styles, genres;
3. causa efficiens – techniques, musical instruments, hardware, creative activity (creativity, musical thinking);
4. causa finalis – performances, productions, functional use, distribution etc.

Knakkergaard analyses the consequences of digitisation (virtualisation) of causes, and he finds that they all reside outside of the real (physical) world and are therefore mere simulations. He concludes that digital technology is not a medium in the sense of either form or content. It is merely a basic condition or status, and its functioning is fictitious. Digitality does not mediate anything, but instead it constructs/reconstructs. It creates a self-containing non-material reality (simulacrum) that is parallel to our physical world.

4.6 On the aesthetics of the digital artefact

With the arrival of the first digital computers in the 1930s, the aesthetic of the industrial era has been gradually replaced by the aesthetic of the digital. Likewise, just as the arts of the industrial era are conditioned by the functionality of the machine and by social aspects of its practice, in the information era the principles of the organisation, distribution, and perception of information are becoming the basic features of artistic creation. Besides traditional constitutive elements such as mass, energy, space, time, form, and entropy, some of the characteristics of the industrial era already described by Marx are persisting into the present era according to Sean Cubitt.[130] For example, there is the understanding of the machine as "dead labour", i.e. the accumulated scientific and technical knowledge and skill of previous generations. The result is the anonymous objectivity of the machine. The same principle can also be applied to the tools of the post-industrial era, e.g. to hardware or software. Other characteristics are new according to Cubitt. Firstly, there is the principle of internal non-identity, whereby every digital artefact is both code and an execution of that code, i.e. a picture, sound, animation etc. Furthermore, there is the principle of ephemerality. As the author of the study points out, new media are apparently less permanent and reliable than the old ones. The idea that digital productions are infinitely copyable and sustainable is utopian because, as it

---

130   CUBITT, Sean. Aesthetic of the Digital. In PAUL, Christiane (ed.). *A Companion to Digital Art*. Hoboken: John Wiley & Sons Inc., 2016, pp. 265–280.

turns out, even during digital copying there are small changes to the code that lead to the irreversible degradation of the result. A third quality of a digital artefact is its unknowability. The code is designed to be read by machines, not people. According to Cubitt, the fourth condition that binds the first three together and makes sense of them is subjectivity, i.e. the presence of the human subject as the author or public. The presence of mankind is a basic feature of the digital aesthetic. This point would seem to be a tautology because Greek *aisthēsis* necessarily requires the presence of a perceiving human being. This is not just a matter of mere perception, but also of the construction of meaning, which is a manifestation of thought. There is also a current boom in artificial intelligence in music, which raises a number of disturbing questions about the place of humans in the process of computer-assisted creativity.

4.7 Causes of the materialisation of music

Music is one of the most abstract media of artistic expression.[131] Its material is nothing but the vibration of various materials represented symbolically by notation or by a recording. At the moment when music moved into the environment of digital media, its last ties to material media were broken, and it became an abstract code. The already high degree of abstraction of musical material has been intensified by the deepening dematerialisation of other components of musical communication (performers, instruments, works, recording media, distribution channels etc.). The various kinds of physical materialisation of music in other media may be a consequence of the unbearableness of music's abstraction. Another necessary condition leading to music being put into a fixed, material form is its ephemerality, being tied to a living author or performer. If music is not notated or recorded, it dies with the person who made it. There is also its connection to a concrete position in time and space. As an ephemeral gesture in time and space, music has always been forced to find other media into which it could impress its form and escape its own ephemeral transience. Whether this involved human memory, a stone, paper, or other media, there was always one purpose: for music to become immortal. Music has projected its symbolic representation into other visual media than just notation, for example in paintings, sculpture, or architecture (which we can understand under certain circumstances as a sculpture inside out).

Other causes for the necessity of materialising music might be said to be the possibility of its manipulation or its availability. It is only possible to manipulate music indirectly through musical instruments or the intellectual manipulation of its symbolic representation. In one of my earlier studies,[132] I refer to Iannis Xenakis and his comments about the need to translate temporal events into space, or to translate

---

131   Chapters 4.7 and 4.8 are a revised version of my text published in HLAVÁČKOVÁ, Jitka and VOJTĚCHOVSKÝ, Miloš (eds.). *Sounds, Codes, Images.* Praha: ArtMap, 2020, pp. 63–72.

132   See FLAŠAR, Martin. *Poème électronique, 1958. Le Corbusier, E. Varèse, I. Xenakis.* Brno: Masarykova univerzita, 2012. Chapter 5.

audible phenomena into the area of visual perception. Xenakis tries to differentiate between musical structures existing "in time" and musical structures existing "outside of time".[133] Xenakis compares musical notation to photography (just as Stravinsky spoke of his composition *Piano Rag Music* as a "snapshot of jazz"), where the individual entities, the relationships between them, and the forms that they create exist basically outside of time. He compares them to traces in our memory, but that is not precise because compared with paper, human memory succumbs to time far more easily. Xenakis says the geographical map of these records of memory is located "outside of time". This applies, for example, to scales, the church modes, morphological units, and higher-level structures. They create systems of abstract rules like mathematics or logic. These entities are directly available, and access to them is not dependent on the linear flow of time. In relation to sounding music and music theory or terminology, the paradox of a temporal dichotomy arises: music participates in space both in time and outside of time. According to Xenakis, however, working with temporal structures is possible only outside of time thanks to their capturing (imaging) in memory (or in any other storage medium). In this process, there is a translation of temporal events into space. Only in this way (outside of time) can we work with material that is based on the flowing of time. In this way, he draws attention to what is *de facto* one of the greatest discoveries of the 20th century, namely spatiotemporal relativity. The result is the observation that temporal art is created by the intellectual manipulation of space.

4.8 Forms of the materialisation of music

The media of the materialisation of music can take various forms. This usually involves translation into different artforms like painting, sculpture, architecture etc. In my dissertation, I dealt with Edgard Varèse's approach to music as being like an approach to a spatial body, where it is possible to work rationally with its form and movement in space. For Varèse, sound is a material that is organised in a four-dimensional continuum on the principle of "metrical simultaneity".[134] Using today's terminology, in his case we would speak of a three-dimensional projection of sound in space. At the inception of these ideas is the concept of a mass of sound as a body that is based on the visual arts. Varèse's first ideas about sound use visual analogies, discussing curves and straight lines of sound, then later he moves on from a two- to a three-dimensional conception.[135]

In the case of abstract art, such ideas are not unique. Meda Mládková, the curator of the works of the founder of Czech school of abstract art František Kupka, explains the painter's obsession with music: "*I experienced many times how*

133 XENAKIS, Iannis. *Formalized Music*, op. cit., 1992, p. 264.

134 BATTIER, Marc. A Constructivist Approach to the Analysis of Electronic Music and Audio Art – between Instruments and Faktura. *Organised Sound* 8(3), Cambridge University Press, pp. 249–255.

135 Cf. relevant passages in FLAŠAR, Martin. *Poème électronique, 1958 : Le Corbusier, E. Varèse, I. Xenakis.* 1st edition, Brno: Masarykova univerzita, 2012.

unhappy he was when he did not have batteries for the radio because he always wanted music playing when he was painting. Not just classical music, but also jazz later on, [...] what Kupka wanted was for a painting to sound like music."[136] Like his contemporaries, he was seeking universal principles valid across individual artistic genres. The movement was called Orphism or Orphic Cubism. G. Apollinaire gave the movement its name in 1912 based on paintings by Robert Delaunay. In this metaphor, Orfeus figured as a musician, singer, and poet.

> "The artists of Orphism drew inspiration from the analogy of the melody of lines and colours, and they created thereby a kind of polyphony—the harmony of the image disengaged itself from the artist's temperament and subjugated itself to the laws of autonomous composition, like in a musical composition. Emphasis was put on rhythm, and works were richly permeated with musicality on the basis of visual dynamism. [...] Every colour and shading on the canvas played a special role, which was incorporated into geometric forms like notes on the staff of a musical score. It evoked the impression of movement advancing in time in an apparent rotation, as if its rings were spinning and releasing a melody onto the visual surface, drowning out the effect of geometrically defined segments. Orphism was an overall expression of the effort to refine the principle of harmony and figured bass in painting."[137]

What enabled the materialisation of music in a different medium was the consequence of the rise of abstract thinking in the arts of the second decade of the 20th century. What we have in mind is the process of abstraction not only from the imaging (mimetic, pictorial, figurative) function of the visual arts, but also abstraction from the characteristic nomenclature of each individual artistic genre. As a consequence of this, a tendency emerged during the period to search for common denominators or terms that could function across individual artist genres (media). In the relationship between the visual arts (painting) and music, mainly the following features are in common: articulation of movement (gesture in time-space), geometry of form, the principle of harmony (relationship between order and chaos), the principle of contrast between elements, spaces, layers, and rhythm. Again in this context, I would draw attention to correspondence between members of the group Der Blaue Reiter; in a letter to Arnold Schoenberg dated 18 January 1911, Wassily Kandinsky wrote:

> "In your works, you have realised what I have been seeking in music in an entirely indefinite form. The natural passage of individual voices through their own fates, through their own lives in their composition is precisely what I have been trying to achieve in the form of painting. At the moment, there is a strong tendency in painting to achieve 'new'

---

136 FARNÁ, Kateřina. Meda Mládková: *František Kupka byl vznešený a krásný člověk* [online]. [Accessed on 5 Oct. 2014]. Retrieved from: http://www.novinky.cz/kultura/258654-meda-mladkova-frantisek-kup-ka-byl-vzneseny-a-krasny-clovek.html.

137 GLENN, Martina. Orfismus [online]. Final version – 9 June 2009. [Accessed on 4 Oct. 2014]. *Artlist.cz*. Retrieved from: http://www.artmuseum.cz/smery_list.php?smer_id=87.

harmonies by constructive means, while the rhythmic component rests upon an almost geometric form."[138]

Eila Hiltunen's abstract sculpture *Passio Musicae* (1967), a memorial to Jean Sibelius in the Töölö district of Helsinki, can be seen as a specific example of the material representation of music. It consists of about six hundred steel pipes welded into a cluster that can represent Sibelius's music, a stand of birch trees, or the aurora borealis.[139] According to the author, the silver-coloured pipes reflect the changes of the seasons and of daylight, they add reverberation to bird singing, and they are themselves made to produce sound by the wind blowing in from the sea or by the rumble of thunder. In addition, the monument is installed over the head of the observer, so the sky and moving clouds are visible through several gaps in the mass of metal. A paradox of this sculpture is that under pressure from the public, the author had to go back later and supplement the abstract form with a realistic mask of the composer installed a few metres away. The public apparently was unable to accept an abstract monument dedicated to music when the expectation was for a monument dedicated to the composer. This historical lesson can be interpreted as an example of the elusiveness of abstract musical form for the public. Also apparently for this reason, models of the reception of music predominate in its physically represented form, either as the anthropomorphic history of composers and performers or as the history of musical texts (musical palaeography), recordings (phonography), images (iconography), or instruments (organology).

In 1934, Edgard Varèse wrote:

"Music and architecture are the only arts alive today – architecture because of the need of it, and out of which an aesthetic sense will grow; music because it is the one art capable of reaching the masses. Architecture, however, does not necessarily crystallize the tendency of the day."[140]

Such a comparison of music and architecture is rather atypical of Varèse. More frequently, he found analogies between sound and the visual arts or in relation to natural processes. Thoughts about the relations between music and architecture appear more prominently with Varèse's coworker in the 1950s, Iannis Xenakis. A representative project along these lines was the Dominican monastery La Tourette near Lyon (1953–1960), which he designed jointly with Le Corbusier. Xenakis enhanced the brutalist design of the monastery by adding a transparent ambulatorium with partitions of variable density and window heights with "pans de verre ondulatoires".

---

138   *Der blaue Reiter: Dokumente einer geistigen Bewegung.* Leipzig: Verlag Philipp Reclam jun., 1986, p. 283. Cf. FLAŠAR, M., HORÁKOVÁ, J. and MACEK, P. *Umění a nová média.* Brno: Masarykova univerzita, 2011, p. 31.

139   Eila Hiltunen [online]. [Accessed on 5 Oct. 2014]. Retrieved from: http://www.eilahiltunen.net/monument.html.

140   In *Varèse and Contemporary Music*, Trend, May-June, 1934, pp. 124–128. Quoted in OUELLETTE, Fernand. *A biography of Edgard Varèse.* Translated from the French by Derek Coltman. New York: Orion Press, 1968, p. 125.

Fig. 6 a–c Eila Hiltunen: *Passio Musicae*. Jean Sibelius Monument, Helsinki. Photo: Martin Flašar.

Fig. 7 a, b Iannis Xenakis: Undulating glass panels in the ambulatorium of the Dominican priory La Tourette (France). Source: www.archdaily.com/96824/.

He calculated their proportions using the Modulor system, allowing the glass façade to give the illusion of musical motion.

He then employed the principle used to design these architectural elements in his composition *Metastaseis* (premiered in 1955 in Donaueschingen). The score of that composition for large orchestra uses an extreme division of parts down to the individual instruments. The instruments are led in straight lines in long glissandos that cross each other, creating linear planes in the score. Xenakis than employed these two-dimensional sound spaces for projections into three-dimensional space, and he created the design for a pavilion on their basis.[141] The goal of the design was the elimination of the maximum share of architecture in the multimedia work. In the attempt to dematerialise the pavilion's architecture as much as possible, Le Corbusier conceived it as a mere "vessel" that would contain light, sound, movement, and colours. Later, Xenakis explained his efforts as follows:

> "[I] need to consider sound and music as a vast potential reservoir in which a knowledge of the laws of thought and the structured creations of thought may find a completely new medium of materialization, i.e., of communication."[142]

For Xenakis, sound, music, and architecture are just various media of materialisation that enable communication. The media make possible the materialisation of knowledge of the laws of thought and of structured creations of the mind.

4.9 The return of the performer

As we have already mentioned and as Knakkergaard has pointed out, with the arrival of analogue and later of digital recording and sound processing, the need has been eliminated for the presence of the performer and instrument in a single production-reception spatiotemporal framework. With the virtualisation of the instrument, there has been a major change to the author-work relationship, but also to the work-listener relationship. The production of music no longer requires physical contact; hardware has been replaced by software.[143] Music is not made physically, but instead mentally. The more software functions we have available, the more mental activity is required. Music software takes away the possibility of absolute control over the material by offering prefabricated models of thinking and sound manipulation. Simon Emmerson pointed out a similar risk, saying that the arrival of electronic technologies meant the displacement of the human body and instrument, which has been replaced by a number of possibilities ranging from the use of signals from the human brain (e.g. Alvin Lucier and his use of an amplified electroencephalogram (EEG) in his *Music for Solo Performer*, 1965) to entirely immersive types of instruments (e.g. John Cage and David Tudor: *Variations V*, 1965).[144]

A reaction to this situation has been the return of the live performer to electroacoustic music. This has at least three causes:

1. To let listeners understand the causality of sound events ("what made that sound effect") → live electronics.

---

141   Cf. relevant passages in FLAŠAR, op. cit., 2012.

142   XENAKIS, I. *Formalized Music*, op. cit. Preface, p. IX.

143   TAYLOR, op. cit., p. 110.

144   EMMERSON, Simon (ed.). *Music, Electronic Media and Culture*. Ashgate, 2000, p. 195.

2. The availability of computational operations in real time such as sound synthesis, sound modification, and sound diffusion.
3. Interaction of a human with technology in real time → interactive performance.

Emmerson identifies two basic categories of new physical interfaces:

1. Controllers operated directly by the actions of a performer. They monitor and measure physical action (transforming of haptic events into sonic events; transforming of movement in space with the use of remote sensors based on ultrasound, lasers etc.; amplification of the human gesture).
2. Equipment controlled by sound. These devices analyse the resultant sound being produced during a performance with the use of technologies like monitoring the sound envelope (envelope tracking), spectral analysis in real time, or measuring the components of sound. The result of this analysis is then used to control the production or processing of sound.

> "We no longer assert our human presence only through hitting, scraping and blowing the objects around us, but through reasserting our power over the new medium—and using it as source. To do this we need clearly to perceive that the medium is the medium, that is far from making it transparent (as our acousmatic artists have previously advocated) quite the opposite is the case."[145]

The cause of the return of the human being to music is, to put it bluntly, mankind itself. Music without the visible presence of a human being loses its causal connection to mankind; it is virtual, non-human music. According to Emmerson, human presence in technologically produced music can take two main forms:

1. The physical presence of a human being directly when the music is being made (action and behaviour) - amplification of gesture.
2. Psychological presence - technical music being made on the basis of a person's will, choices, and intentions instead of physical human presence. However, the distinctions between the composer, performer, and listener may be blurred, and choices and construction within the framework of the act of listening become an act of actual composition.[146]

4.10 Individualised musical interfaces

The development of new, individualised interfaces for electroacoustic music is yet another of the possible ways out of the crisis of depersonalised acousmatic computer music. In music history so far, we have not encountered the practice of

---

145 EMMERSON, op. cit., p. 212.

146 Ibid., pp. 212–213; Cf. EMMERSON, Simon. *Living Electronic Music.* Routledge, Ashgate, 2007. Chapter *Living Presence*, pp. 2–3.

making individualised instruments very often. Musicians have usually used already existing instruments or have attempted to make instruments of their own imitating common, functional models. The practice of artists themselves being the maker or co-maker of musical instruments is relatively unusual. The areas of musical culture in which these tendencies have been historically most apparent are folk music and experimental music. We could explain the creation of new electronic interfaces as the expansion of influence of individualisation from compositions and interpretation towards musical instruments (interfaces). Individualisation is a characteristic sign of the post-industrial era, when individual products can be adapted to the wishes of an individual, who need not work with a prefabricated and standardised product set up for a broad target group of users. As has been shown by John Richards,[147] we can understand the independent development of the musical interface as part of the compositional or performance process. In this country, Dominik Oslej has devoted himself to the question of alternative touch user interfaces in the production of the digital era in a study that bears that title.[148] The result of the new development is the digital musical instrument (DMI). This involves a system for the creation of music using computerised digital synthesis of sound, with the hardware form of the player's interface using some type of sensor technology. In this system, the controlling interface and the sound synthesis are usually physically separated. The link between gestural action and musical response is secured through mapping of virtual functions on a physical controller.[149] This, then, is a combination of the aforementioned principles: software and hardware, virtual and physical sound manipulation.

Oslej assumes two DMI typologies, and from among them we are choosing the more comprehensive variant according to Miranda and Wanderley:[150]

1. the class of acoustical instruments augmented by the use of sensors;
2. the class of gestural controllers modelled after the control surfaces of acoustical instruments with the goal of fully reproducing their basic properties;
3. the class of controllers inspired by already existing instruments or instruments designed to overcome the limitations of the original models instead of trying to completely reproduce them;
4. the class of alternative controllers not clearly resembling existing instruments.

Oslej asserts that alternative interfaces have been outpaced by traditional electronic interfaces such as keyboards because they still have only briefly been under development and they lack standardisation (and therefore get limited support

---

147　See chapter 5.4.3.2.

148　OSLEJ, Dominik. *Alternatívne dotykové rozhrania v hudobnej produkcii digitálnej éry.* Master's thesis. Supervisor: Mgr. Martin Flašar, Ph.D. Brno: Masarykova univerzita, 2015.

149　Ibid., pp. 11–12.

150　MIRANDA, Eduardo R. and WANDERLEY, Marcelo M. *New Digital Musical Instruments: Control and Interaction Beyond the Keyboard.* Middleton, Wisconsin: A-R Editions, 2006. Preface, p. XX.

from manufacturers) and the support of pedagogues. This, however, brings us back tautologically to their basic characterisation, which is supposed to be an alternative to mainstream musical instruments and interfaces.

As was the case with analogue *musique concrète*, digital computer music has also served as a laboratory of the necessary conditions for what society is willing to accept as music. From an anthropological perspective,[151] music serves not only as a medium of communication, but also a wide variety of functions for social integration, validation, and stabilisation. It is also the object of physical actions and reactions toho. If we replace one of the parts of music's communication model with a medium that is a mere representation of direct, live action, there is a weakening of the authenticity of experiencing music that is communicated through agency.

The mediatisation and representation of music of the 20th century have characteristically been dealt with in terms of the developmental arch that we have tried to describe in this chapter. The departure point of digitisation as the ultimate form of abstraction of already abstract music (sound art), which has necessarily provoked defensive opposition in the form of strengthened calls for a return to the live performer, real instruments, and the ritual of the authentically shared listening experience.

---

151   Cf. MERRIAM, A. P. *The Anthropology of Music*. Evanston: Northwestern University Press, 1964, pp. 209–226.

Chapter 5

Musical Thinking under the Influence of New Technologies

5.1 Techno-utopian and techno-optimistic concepts

Techno-utopian concepts attribute to technology a maximum or maximally positive part in the production of music. Their characteristic feature is the legitimisation of current changes by means of the future. In the music history of the first half of the 20th century, we immediately find several examples of the future serving as a means of legitimising the musical thinking of the present. That tendency has been closely tied to the spirit of modernism calling for progress and originality as consequences of the Enlightenment concept of rationalism. Soon after the beginning of the 20th century, we find a powerful wave of confidence in technical progress applied to the process of musical creation. The concept of faith acquires an important function in this process. Unlike science, of course, faith does not rely on the positivistic evidence of reality. The constructions (even if rational) are presented as dogmas that are to be adopted or followed uncritically. In view of their radical dogmatism, certain individual approaches to poetics, schools, and movements of the first half of the 20th century are closer to faith than to science, such as Feruccio Busoni's essay *Entwurf der neuen Ästhetik der Tonkunst* (1907), Luigi Russolo's manifesto *L'Arte dei rumori* (1913), Edgard Varèse's lecture *The Liberation of Sound* (1936), or John Cage's lecture *The Future of Music: Credo* (1937). We sense from them an apparent tendency to justify the need for changes to contemporary music with visions of the music of the future. The problem is that their positions are largely based on a utopian faith in the future.

John Cage formulates his musical poetics using the word "Credo" ("I believe") in the title. Neither Feruccio Busoni nor Luigi Russolo use logical arguments in their manifestos, in which they announce the need for introducing new instruments, new musical material etc. They do not explain why their particular innovations should become the future of music. It is characteristic of the situation at the time that Schoenberg told his pupil Josef Rufer in 1921 that by the discovery of dodecaphony (of which we now know he was neither the only nor the first inventor) he had ensured the supremacy of German music for the next hundred years.[152] This statement by a rationalistic composer sounds more like the words of a dogmatist striving for influence. It is surprising that Schoenberg, fascinated by mathematical and rational musical constructions, would let himself get carried away and make such a childish proclamation. Moreover, as we now know, the consequences of Schoenberg's methods had ceased to be of interest to the majority of composers just thirty years later. Despite his importance in music history, his assertion can be regarded as myopic. It also raises disturbing questions: why should a composer strive for any kind of supremacy in music, and why should German music dominate other musical cultures?

Arthur Honegger's *Mouvement Symphonique No. 1*, later given the title *Pacific 231* (1923), is an example of musical thinking enchanted by technology. The music's mechanical rhythms seem to be based on the movement of the steam engine powering the locomotive after which the piece is named. Honegger declared that he had always been a passionate lover of locomotives, which he regarded as living beings (a statement that sounds as if lifted directly out of Marinetti's manifesto of futurism), and which he loved just as others love women or horses.[153] Later, however, the composer called into question the original programme of his program *Mouvement Symphonique*, in which he discusses in a futuristic style "the quiet breathing of the machine at rest", instead saying that the title *Pacific 231* came into being quite randomly after the music had been written as a polyphonic tribute to Bach's counterpoint.[154] According to Roger, it is very likely that Honegger was caught off guard by the number of oversimplified interpretations that attributed a purely illustrative character to his piece.[155] The paradox of the composition is that while the tempo slows down, the real rate of surface motion accelerates, the writing becomes denser, and the music builds up dynamically. The excerpt from the score shown below is from the very end of the movement, where we find the whole orchestra playing regular ostinato figures. The motion of high-pitched instruments in groups of four sixteenth notes stands in opposition to the triplet motion of the low voices, creating a simple polyrhythm.

What does the phrase "contemporary music" actually mean to modern composers? When hearing Iannis Xenakis's newly composed work titled *Metastaseis* (1953–1954), Edgard Varèse said "this is the music of our time",[156] but the statement remains a bit mysterious. Does it mean the same thing as, for example, Benedetto Marcello's *Teatro alla moda*, i.e. musical expression of the general taste of its time? What Varèse is talking about here is not music as a collective norm, but instead music that reflects the individual experience of a person living in the 1950s in Europe in the midst of the Cold War and the race to attain technological superiority. The compositional

---

152   Cf. RUFER, Josef. *Das Werk Arnold Schönbergs*. Kassel, 1959, p. 26.

153   ROGER, Nichols. *The Harlequin Years: Music in Paris 1917–1929*. University of California Press, 2002, p. 233.

154   HONEGGER, Arthur. *I Am a Composer*. London: Faber, 1966, p. 101.

155   ROGER, op. cit., p. 233.

156   DELALANDE, François. *Entretiens avec Xenakis: „Il faut être constamment un immigré"*. Paris: INA-Buchet/Chastel, Pierre Zech éditeur, 1997, p. 56.

Fig. 8 A. Honegger: *Pacific 231.* Score. Paris : Maurice Senart, 1924. Plate S.6680, bars 199-201. Source: http://petruccilibrary.ca.

technique of *Metastaseis* is derived from geometry, and its structure is influenced by electronic technologies, but the work employs traditional instruments. Its sound world tends towards noise expressed by musical means. In view of the tempestuous reaction to the premiere at the Donaueschinger Musiktagen in 1955, it is quite clear that Xenakis's music was not in accordance with the tastes of even a specialised public. In the music history of the 20th century, there are many cases of audiences not accepting new music as contemporary. The public often expects that new music will be older than it really is, meaning that the expectation is for innovation within the context of established aesthetic and formal norms. Of course, truly great composers usher in a change of style, aesthetic views, or expressive resources. They come up with a new system of thinking that is only later to become a referential framework.

The 20th century discovered noise and sound not only in the form of an appropriating mimetic principle (which is already familiar to us from the caccie of the 14th century and the madrigal of the 16th), but also as a full-fledged material that can be freely manipulated with the use of newly emerging technologies. Milan Kundera in his essay *Hudba a hluk*[157] (Music and Noise) gives examples from the music of the 20th century that most clearly exhibit the tendency to work with sounds not in the character of tones: the men's chorus *Sedmdesát tisíc* (The Seventy Thousand, 1909) by Leoš Janáček, *Les noces* (1914–1923) by Igor Stravinsky, the piano suite *Out of Doors* (1926) by Béla Bartók, and Bartók's *First Piano Concerto*. And finally, there are compositions by Varèse and Xenakis: *"these images of sound worlds, objective but non-existent, told me about being liberated from aggressive and burdensome human subjectivity; they told me of the tender non-human beauty of the earth at a time before or after people were passing through it."*[158]

An analogous example from the late 20th century is *Different Trains* (1988) by Steve Reich. The programme of the three-movement cycle for four string quartets (three recorded and one playing live) is about people's fates in connection with trains before, during, and after the Second World War. In the score, he writes that for him in the years 1939–42, a train meant the adventure of travelling accompanied by his guardian between his divorced parents in New York and Los Angeles, but very different trains were crossing Europe in those days.

> "While these trips were exciting and romantic at the time, I now look back and think that, if I had been in Europe during this period, as a Jew I would have had to ride very different trains."[159]

---

157   KUNDERA, Milan. *O hudbě a románu*. Brno: Atlantis, 2014, p. 24.

158   Ibid., p. 26.

159   REICH, Steve. Note by the Composer. In *Different Trains for String Quartet and Pre-recorded Performance Tape*. Score [online]. Hendon Music, Boosey and Hawkes, 1988. [Accessed on 31 Jan. 2019]. Retrieved from: http://edoc.site.

Fig. 9 Steve Reich: *Different Trains.* Score. Boosey and Hawkes (Hendon Music), [1988]. HPS II68, p. 11, bars 113-118.

By a method similar to Janáček's speech melodies (as the composer actively acknowledges), he tries both to capture the psychology of the passengers and to depict the times with brief excerpts from sentences. He works with speech melodies of authentic passengers: his guardian, the steward in the train, and three speakers who survived the Holocaust and moved to the USA. We can therefore call his string quartet a programmatic and documentary composition.

The melodic line of speech is doubled by instruments, disengaging the melody from speech, and retaining its purely musical meaning in a sounding structure.

Like Honegger, Reich's departure point is the mechanical kinetics of a machine, which he harmonises. However, he balances this with a human element in the form of spoken phrases, which lend the mechanical (impersonal) music a very personal content and determine its melody.

These two compositions belong to different periods of the 20th century, but they have in common a basic structural principle: they are inspired by a mechanical device. The kinetics of a machine become the controlling factor of the musical structure and determine the musical thinking.

5.2 Techno-realistic conceptions of music

> "The great problem of our time is to restore modern man's balance and wholeness: to give him the capacity to command the machines he has created instead of becoming their helpless accomplice and passive victim; to bring back, into the very heart of our culture, that respect for the essential attributes of personality, its creativity and autonomy, which Western man lost at the moment he displaced his own life in order to concentrate on the improvement of the machine."
>
> Lewis Mumford: *Art and Technics*[160]

Until the 19th century, mechanical technologies existed in the realm of music solely to support its production. All musical instruments were being made as sophisticated technological tools for creating music, and mechanised printing created the foundation for collective musical memory. No later than by the 19th century, technologies had gradually begun to replace additional links in the chain of musical communication. Performers could be replaced by musical automatons, and the space of a concert hall or opera theatre was replaced by a phonograph recording or (a few decades later) by radio. The collective experience of a societal gathering found a parallel in isolated, intimately individualised listening. This change led to a weakening of shared culture[161] that had been the foundation of European and other civilisations. Technologies have successively conquered all aspects of musical experience. Surprisingly, until about the 1950s the public remained relatively undisturbed by these enormous technological changes. It was finally technologies like magnetic tape, oscillators, noise generators, filters, loudspeakers, or microphones used for the processing and production of music that opened the eyes (or ears) of the public, which suddenly found itself in a new cultural paradigm. The three basic approaches to technology in the musical thinking of the 20th and early 21st centuries that we are working with reflect the relationships and attitudes of creative musicians to technology. The true challenge of our time is finding an equilibrium between the world of mankind and the world of technology. For our purposes, we call this balanced approach of compromise "techno-realism".

5.2.1 Technology versus intention, invention, and imagination

A realistic approach to technology in the process of musical creation means recognising and grasping its true place and value in that process. Firstly, there is technology's instrumental function, whereby it becomes a means of attaining creative goals set by a person's intention, invention, and imagination. While technology becomes a framework or a structuring factor of the composer's musical thinking, as Ortega y Gasset points out, human free will assigns technology its meaning.

---

160   MUMFORD, Lewis. *Art and Technics*. New York: Columbia University Press, 1952, p. 11.

161   SCRUTON, Roger. *An Intelligent Person's Guide to Modern Culture*. London: Duckworth, 1998.

"[...] the meaning and cause of technology lies outside of it; this is the same as the employment that one gives to one's free powers after they have been released by technology. The initial mission of technology is this: to give man freedom to remain free to be himself."[162]

The purpose of musical technology is the liberations of composers' thinking and the realisation of their creative freedom. Technology should become a tool for the liberation of their intention, invention, and imagination. At the same time, one cannot see in technology itself an area of realisation of music's meaning. European music has been and will always be individualistic, and as such it has been the realisation of the individual artistic intent of the composer. The existence of a musical instrument, a compositional technique, or a style does not guarantee the creation of an original musical composition. Invention and imagination precede the intent that is expressed or realised through technology. What need concern us is not the absence or regression of technology, but rather the absence of human and artistic intent, which would mean the absence of meaning in the music itself:

> "'Europe is suffering from the exhaustion of its ability to desire.' And this eclipse, which has brought the programme of life under fire, has ushered in the throttling and reversal of technology, which will have no idea know what and whom to serve. [...] the man of today does not know what to be: he lacks the imagination to invent the content of his own life."[163]

Techno-optimists and utopians of the modern era assumed that music can be revived by discovering new instruments and compositional techniques, but they may have forgotten to pose the far more serious question concerning the meaning and mission of European music. While composers of the 19th century are viewed by the public as executors of a *force majeure*, realising their talents and employing their genius, composers of the 20th century had to be satisfied with the role of active musicians, conductors, pedagogues, or, in exceptional cases, figures who are subsidised from private or state funds. A symptomatic reaction to the development of the standing of the composer of art music in the mid-20th century appears in a 1951 interview with Arthur Honegger, who drew attention to the internal contradiction faced by composers of that period:

> "I am convinced of the end of music in the near future, yet I am a professor of composition. I have thirty-seven students at the École Normale de Musique. My class always begins— and you can confirm this—with a little speech of which this is roughly the substance: 'Gentlemen, do you sincerely wish to become composers of music? Have you reflected carefully on what awaits you? If you write music, you will not be paid and you will not earn a living. If your father can afford to support you, then nothing prevents you from

---

162   ORTEGA Y GASSET, José, op. cit., p. 41.

163   Ibid., p. 42.

putting black marks on paper. You will learn that, wherever you go, what you value above all other things will have but a secondary importance for others; they will show no impatience to discover you and your sonata.'"[164]

An important impulse for the revitalisation of European music after the Second World War was the emergence of the young generation of composers born after the First World War (K. Stockhausen, P. Boulez, I. Xenakis et al.). Their tendency to distance themselves from music with a subjectivistic, emotional basis led to the use of rationalistic composition methods. This required either an education in technology or the natural sciences or at least an inclination towards them. In combination with new technologies for the generation, processing, and storage of sound, the development of which had been accelerated by the Second World War, there arose an entirely new musical aesthetic based on electronic media.[165]

5.2.2 Edgard Varèse and his conception of the role of technology

Having just turned 30, Edgard Varèse formulated his aesthetic convictions for the New York Morning Telegraph. His search for new instruments, however, was not by its nature a utopian vision of redeeming music through current technologies. Varèse was very well aware of the subordinate position of technology in the process of musical creativity.

"Our musical alphabet must be enriched. We also need new instruments very badly. The futurists (Marinetti and his noise-artists) have made a serious mistake in this respect. Instruments, after all, must only be temporary means of expression. Musicians should take up this question in deep earnest with the help of machinery specialist. I have always felt the need of new medium of expression in my own work. I refuse to submit myself only to sounds that have already been heard. What I am looking for are new technical mediums which can lend themselves to every expression of thought and can keep up with thought."[166]

Here, Varèse affirms that the musical idea takes precedence over technologies, which must be understood here merely as a temporary means of expression. A year later in Picabia's magazine 391, he published the manifesto *Que la musique sonne*, in which he formulates this position quite unambiguously:

---

164 HONEGGER, Arthur. *I Am a Composer*. London: Faber, 1966, p. 31.

165 I have addressed the problem of electroacoustic music in more detail in the publication *Elektroakustická hudba* [online]. 1st edition. Brno: Masarykova univerzita, 2015. [Accessed on 9 Jan. 2018]. Elportál. Retrieved from: http://is.muni.cz/elportal/?id=1308636.

166 OUELLETTE, Fernand. *Edgard Varèse*. Translated from the French by Derek Coltman. New York: The Orion Press, 1966, p. 46.

"My dream is of instruments that will obey my thought—and which, by bringing about a flowering of hitherto unsuspected timbres, will lend themselves to the combinations it will please me to impose on them and bow themselves to the demands of my inner rhythm."[167]

I have dealt with this matter in great detail in an earlier book, to which I shall refer below.[168]

An example of the balancing of human (subjective) and mechanical (objective) principles is Varèse's symphonic poem *Déserts* (1954). In it, Varèse used recordings of sounds from industrial manufacturing, mixed using the methods of *musique concrète* into three electroacoustic interpolations inserted in a symphonic movement being played live. The composition is historically important not only for its combining of live music with *musique concrète*, specifically a large orchestra and a magnetic tape, but also for attempting to establish a balance between two entirely different soundscapes. The audio image produced by the orchestra does not actually differ strikingly from the industrial interpolations. The two sound worlds form a monolithic whole that is an expression of the search for balance between the world of technology and live music.

5.2.3 Pierre Boulez: A mage and a plumber

Soon after the appearance of electroacoustic music, it became institutionalised at radio and television stations and also at universities. Perhaps the most explicit example of state interest in this kind of music in Europe was the Parisian institute IRCAM (Institut de Recherche et Coordination Acoustique/Musique). After its founding in 1977, French president Georges Pompidou entrusted the composer Pierre Boulez with conceptual and administrative leadership of the institute.

Boulez devoted himself to electroacoustic music in two large waves: in the 1950s and at the turn of the 1980s and '90s. One of his key texts concerning the relationship between technology and composition is *Invention/Recherche* (1977, published in English as *Technology and the Composer*).[169] According to Boulez, invention cannot exist on an abstract level, but comes from contact with the music of the past. Nonetheless, invention faces a number of problems: he concentrates mainly on the relationship between the *concept* (the composer's vision) and the *realisation* of the idea in sound. This divergence of concept and material (to which employed technologies or media also belong) leads to an imbalance in which the material and idea develop independently of each other.

---

167 VARÈSE, Edgard. Que la musique sonne. 391, No. 5, June 1917, New York, p. 2, quoted in OUELLETTE, op. cit., p. 39.

168 FLAŠAR, Martin. *Poème électronique, 1958: Le Corbusier, E. Varèse, I. Xenakis.* Brno: Masarykova univerzita, 2012. Spisy Masarykovy univerzity v Brně, Filozofická fakulta.

169 BOULEZ, Pierre. Technology and the Composer. *Leonardo*, 1978, Vol. 11, No. 1, pp. 59-62. Retrieved from: www.jstor.org/stable/1573509.

According to Boulez, the technologies for recording, storing, transmitting, and reproducing (microphones, loudspeakers, amplifiers, magnetic tapes) have arrived at a point where they have betrayed their original goal, which had been faithful reproduction. According to him, reproduction technologies increasingly tend towards autonomy and an attempt to imprint their own image onto existing music at the expense of efforts towards the most faithful reproduction possible. This critical observation belongs under the heading of technological determinism. Another point that Boulez refers to is the dynamism of development of musical technologies, which are constantly changing and are subject to the inexorable law of motion and development under the constant pressure of the market. In this context, one can apply the term "liquidity" used later by Zygmunt Bauman.[170] According to him, the term characterises the arts of a period of liquid modernism, in which time flows but does not make progress. This involves a status of constant transformation without a vision for a conclusion, a sequence of constant new beginnings.

"Liquid modernity may be characterized as a state in which the important oppositions which constituted the framework of early, solid modernity have been cancelled: oppositions between creative and destructive arts, between learning and forgetting, between forward and backward steps. The pointer has been removed from the arrow of time; so you have an arrow, but without a pointer."[171]

According to Boulez, a paradoxical reaction to the constant supply of new technologies in music is the retreat to historical music. According to this paradoxical theory, musical historicism is a reaction against the radicalness, changeability, and elusiveness of new music, but one can only partly agree with this assertion. Musical historicism is a much older phenomenon (by about a century) than the arrival of new technologies in the 20th century. From the 1920s, Schoenberg and his pupils were attempting a compromise, combining new music with old music by the use of old forms (the suite, passacaglia etc.) and contrapuntal techniques, and Stravinsky went down a similar path. If historicism was an immediate reaction to the post-war New Music or electroacoustic music, we would have to observe an increase of such production no later than by the 1950s. The events of the music of the 1970s (whether post-modern composition trends such as polystylism or the flourishing of informed interpretation of early music) would have been a rather late reaction that might be more suitably called the exhaustion of New Music.

According to Boulez, the music of the 1970s found itself at the crossroads of two different paths. The first is a conservative historicism that, if not completely blocking invention, clearly diminishes it by providing no new material needed for expression or regeneration. Instead, it creates barriers and hinders the orientation from the composer to the performer or more generally from the idea to the material. Offering a second path are progressive technologies, the power

---

170   BAUMAN, Zygmunt. Liquid Arts. *Theory Culture & Society*, 2007, 24, pp. 117–126.

171   Ibid, p. 121.

of expression and development of which have been reduced to the dissemination of material resources, which may or may not be in accordance with the actual musical idea, as was said above. Boulez points out that the character of technology is dictated by inventors, engineers, and technicians who are pursuing strictly scientific interests in their search for new processes. Musicians generally feel put off by all things technical and scientific, and their education and culture have given them neither the proficiency nor the willingness to solve problems of this kind. Musicians' reactions to new technologies are either to make selections from the samples that are available to them or to work at the level of simply achievable manipulation of the material. Rather than raising the question of whether the material is adequate to the idea or whether the idea is compatible with the material, they simply ask whether the material meet their immediate needs. The finding of Boulez's analysis is a need for cooperation between scientists and musicians, which he metaphorically calls a "marriage of fire and water".

"Uncertain just what it is that musicians are demanding from them, and what possible terrain there might be for joint efforts, many scientists opt out in advance, seeing only the absurdity of the situation: that is, a mage reduced to begging for help from a plumber! If, in addition, the mage imagines that the plumber's services are all that he needs, then confusion is total. It is easy to see how hard it will be ever to establish a common language for both technological and musical invention."[172]

In a similar spirit, Ortega y Gasset adds: *"In principle, technology cannot ultimately command or direct things. Its role is enormous and worthy of respect, but unavoidably secondary."*[173]

The outcome of Boulez's idea is the assertion that ultimately, musicians somehow must learn and appropriate the language of technology. Musicians will miss out on the full arsenal of technologies because the preponderance of technology goes beyond musicians' specialisations, but they will still be able to assimilate basic technical procedures and functions. In other words, it is necessary to ensure that musical invention (musical thinking) achieves the creation of the musical material it needs and for musicians to provide the necessary impulse for creating technologies that react flexibly to the musicians' desires and imagination. The process will need to be flexible enough to prevent the extreme rigidity of technological determinism and to provide for the random and the unforeseen.

---

172   BOULEZ, op. cit., p. 61.

173   ORTEGA Y GASSET, op. cit., p. 43.

Boulez actually proposes the following arrangement:

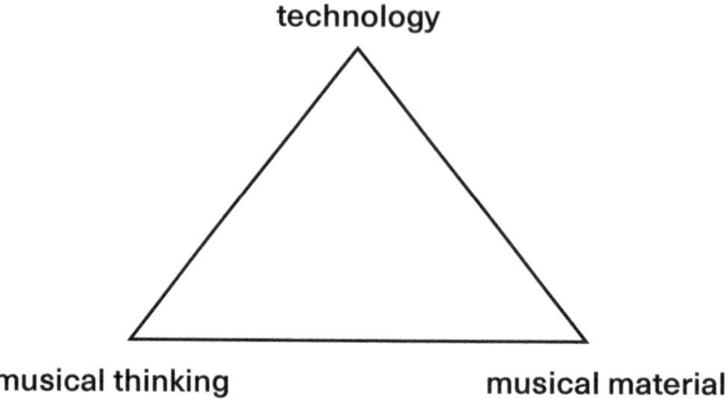

Fig. 10 Diagram of the function of technology in relation to musical thinking
and material according to P. Boulez.

According to him, the logical extension of the material will inspire new ways
of thinking, provoking a very complex game of mirroring between thinking and the
material, with reflections constantly passing back and forth. He uses architecture
as a parallel: new materials brought changes to thinking and to style. If technology
will be sufficiently flexible, it will be possible to realise ideas directly in the material
itself:

"At its limits, one can imagine possible works where material and idea are brought
to coincide by the final, instantaneous operation that gives them a true, provisional
existence—that operation being the activity of the composer, of a performer, or of the
audience itself. Certainly, the finite categories within which we are still accustomed
to evolve will offer less interest when this dizzying prospect opens up: of a stored-up
potential creating instant originality."[174]

At the same time, he adds that only collective effort will lead to this point. No
individual, however talented, can attain the solution of all the problems represented
by the present developments of musical expression. This also explains the need
for the institutionalisation of technology-based music. The result is a cooperative
model of musical production, which will later be superseded by the individualised
(integrated) model of the artist-technician.

---

174   BOULEZ, op. cit., p. 62.

    Chapter 5: **Musical Thinking under the Influence of New Technologies**

5.2.4 Kaija Saariaho: Technologies subjugated to imagination

> "I just wanted my music to sound as I imagined it."
>
> Kaija Saariaho

The approach of the Finnish-French composer Kaija Saariaho (1952–2023) represents one of the major lessons on the use of electronic technology in contemporary composing. She had already begun using electronics as a student at the Sibelius Academy in Helsinki, mainly because of the resulting spatial arrangement of the sound of her compositions, which had been negatively affected by the acoustics of the local concert halls.[175] She interspersed her studies under Magnus Lindberg and other teachers with encounters with Brian Ferneyhough in Freiburg and finally research at Paris's IRCAM. There she became familiar with computer assisted composition (CAC), tape music, and live electronics.[176] Of major importance to her was her encounter with the French spectralists, who prepared their compositional material by the analysis of sound spectra. On the basis of that approach, she developed her own method of working with the partials of tones, including microtonality and even her own notation, which covers a broad range from tones to sound material. Nonetheless, the image and structure of sound have remained at the centre of her attention.

> "Sound quality in electronics is extremely important for me, and for a long time it was not attainable with real-time technology. So when I worked with the voice, I prepared processed treatments in sound files to be triggered at given cues in the score, and I mixed these together with amplification and live electronics, mostly consisting of reverberation. In this way, I could achieve a satisfying blend between instrumental qualities and electronics possibilities."[177]

After technologically insufficient beginnings, real-time technologies began to arrive, fulfilling the composer's ideas of the resulting form of sound processing through live electronics.

Saariaho critically evaluated developments in the field of computer composition in the 1980s, when technological innovations and approaches were rarely being brought together with musically satisfying results. It was like a repeat of the beginnings of *musique concrète*, when technological solutions (or methods) were far ahead of an aesthetically satisfactory result.

---

175 CAMPION, Edmund. Dual Reflections: A Conversation with Kaija Saariaho and Jean-Baptiste Barrière on Music, Art, and Technology. *Computer Music Journal*. MIT Press, 2015.

176 SAARIAHO, Kaija. *Biography* [online]. [Accessed on 1 July 2018]. Retrieved from: http://saariaho.org/biography.

177 CAMPION, op. cit., p. 10.

Musique mixte is probably the most fitting designation for the genre of music that Saariaho creates.[178] In it, she tries to find a balance between live and electroacoustic music. Of major importance to her is a pragmatic approach to technologies, which must be flexible, cheap, and widely available. Electronic (software) solutions and hardware integration are offered to potential performers free of charge online, for example in the form of patches programmed using Max software, instructions for the use of audio technology, sound characteristics etc. This approach is a far cry from the institutional self-consciousness of the 1950s and '60s, when belonging to the right institution was basically equated with a certain degree of mystical initiation. With Saariaho, composing always begins with a concrete idea of the sound for a particular work. Only then does the search for or direct development of technological resources to realise that sound begin, and not the other way around:

> "Kaija has no technical bias in the beginning; therefore, she is not limited by technological constraints. She imagines something musically and we find a way to realize it. Many people are the other way around: They discover a specific tool and then imagine how to use it musically."[179]

Very important to Kaija Saariaho's poetics is the position of compromise in the relationship between the old and the new and also between the natural and the artificial. She says that if we are working with pitches and rhythms, we are involved with the same kind of material as our predecessors. Just like innovations, traditions in music can serve as inspiration for composers, but they must not become limitations on their ideas and creativity:

> "As we can be inspired by history without copying it, we can also find different tools in today's technologies, not be prisoners of them, customize them for our needs, develop them to suit our visions, and create music that was never heard before."[180]

In February 2018, Kaija Saariaho was honoured for her lifetime achievements in the contemporary music category of the BBVA Foundation Frontiers of Knowledge Award. The jury, led by Cambridge University professor emeritus Nicholas Cook, gave her recognition for the ability to link imperceptibly the world of acoustic music and technology. Previous award winners have included Pierre Boulez, Sofia Gubaidulina, György Kurtág, and Steve Reich.[181]

---

178   *Musique mixte* can be defined as the combination of electroacoustic material produced by loudspeakers with purely acoustic instrumental or vocal material. It is divided depending upon the nature of the combined sources and the time when it is taking place (real time, deferred time). See various studies by Vincent Tiffon, e.g. *Musique mixte : Repères historiques. Un diaporama avec la définition et les principaux repères historiques de la musique mixte, sur ariam-idf.com* [online]. [Accessed on 2 July 2018]. 18 Oct. 2012, rev. 28 Aug. 2017. Retrieved from: http://www.ariam-idf.com/sites/default/files/18-support-tiffon.pdf.

179   Ibid., p. 17.

180   Ibid., p. 20.

181   *The BBVA Foundation recognizes Finnish composer Kaija Saariaho for breaking down the divisions between acoustic and electronic music* [online]. [Accessed on 2 July 2018]. Retrieved from: www.bbva.com.

5.3 The technosceptic musical perspective

From the arguments made above, it is clear that one cannot consider music without taking technology into account, just as the visual arts or architecture are unthinkable without technological procedures. As has already been said, music employs technique—i.e. the application of rational procedures—at least in its structuring and distribution. In this instrumental or pragmatic sense, it is not at all possible to eliminate technology from music. In other contexts, however, we can consider the revision of technology's function in music. This especially involves the ontological function, in which technology comes to the forefront in music (usually as an object of mimesis or of worship). In the history of 20th-century music, one can trace a clear shift from the object towards the subject of creation, from *mimēsis* towards *poiēsis*, or from an ontological function of technology in music towards a pragmatic function.[182]

If the hopes of certain composers and musicians for the music of the interwar and early post-war periods were counting on technology as a means of salvation for music of the present through a vision of the future, the development of musical thinking in the decades that followed showed how myopic those visions were.

5.3.1 Technology as theology. Between an ontological and a pragmatic function

In modern compositions, we still find music as a means of depicting or celebrating technology (e.g. A. Mosolov: *The Iron Foundry*, op. 19; B. Martinů: *Le raid merveilleux, Thunderbolt P-47*; A. Honegger: *Pacific 231*; P. Hindemith and K. Weill: *Der Lindberghflug*, L. Hiller and L. Isaacson: *ILLIAC Suite for String Quartet*, K. Stockhausen: *Helicopter Quartet* etc.) springing from the optimism that was developing an enlightenment concept of progress. In the postmodern phase of musical development, we tend to encounter music as a tool for criticism of technology (J. Adams: *Dr. Atomic*, Steve Reich: *Three Tales*). Nonetheless, this shift of ontological function paradoxically does not exclude the use of electronic technology for the realising of these compositions or for their structured role. One might speak of the ironicising of technology because we find ourselves in a vicious circle in which technological means are used for the criticism of technology as such.

The shift of emphasis to the pragmatic function of technology in music amounts to a return of technology from the position of a depicted object to an instrumental role. Technology ceases to be a mimetic object and goes back to being a mere subject expressing artistic intent.

One might give as an example of the modern objectivization of electronic technology in music François Bayle's Acousmonium installed in the O. Messiaen Hall of the Maison de Radio France in Paris. As a kind of virtual orchestra, it became the ultimate expression of efforts towards the incarnation of acousmatic music.

---

182 Cf. FLAŠAR, Martin. Technology or Theology? Music Beyond Technology. *Musicologica Brunensia.* Brno: Masarykova univerzita, 2017, Vol. 52, No. 1, pp. 63–68.

Fig. 11 Acousmonium, O. Messiaen Hall, Radio France, Paris.
Source: https://zengrained.wordpress.com/.
(Photo by L. Ruszka and supplied courtesy of F. Bayle and the GRM.)

In the remediation theory of Bolter and Grusin,[183] the logic of hypermediacy corresponds to these objectivising strategies:

"In the logic of hypermediacy, the artist (or multimedia programmer or web designer) strives to make the viewer acknowledge the medium as a medium and to delight in that acknowledgement. She does so by multiplying spaces and media and by repeatedly redefining the visual and conceptual relationships among mediated spaces – relationships that may range from simple juxtaposition to complete absorption."[184]

Enjoying the secondary aspects of a musical performance is equivalent to the emphasis on the exhibition of technical virtuosity in music from the 18th century until the present. We still find ourselves on the secondary level of the visual quality of music, i.e. of the objects for the production of sound and music, and not on the primary level of the quality of the audible structure.

If we examine the causes for the changing attitudes of composers and musicians towards electronic technologies and the growing scepticism about them in the course of the 20th century, we find in particular the following reasons:

---

183 BOLTER, Jay D. and GRUSIN, Richard A. *Remediation: Understanding New Media*. Cambridge: MIT Press, 2000.

184 Ibid., pp. 41–42.

1. Electronic technologies do not represent a sufficient means of achieving a new sound world. In about the mid-1950s, leading composers of the European avant-garde were vacillating between electroacoustic and purely acoustic music, and in both cases the approaches led primarily to a new sound world. The choice between electroacoustic music and live music often did not end up in electroacoustic music's favour. Examples include Stockhausen's *Gruppen* or *Carré*, Xenakis's *Metastaseis*, and Ligeti's *Apparitions* and *Atmosphères*. Often, this was because of the difficulty of an electronic solution, while a similar result could be achieved by the methods of purely acoustic music as well. Electronic technologies led mainly to the discovery of new timbres or to new methodologies of working with sound material, which enriched composed acoustical music.

2. The communication barrier between technicians and artists remains difficult to bridge. An important factor when considering the use of electronic technologies in the creative process was the lack of shared knowledge between technicians and artists in sound studios, which hindered their communication. The creation of early electroacoustic music routinely faced this problem, and the quality of the music depended on the degree of mutual understanding. For example, there were collaborations between P. Schaeffer and P. Henry at RTF, H. Eimert and Karlheinz Stockhausen at WDR, and W. Tak, S. L. de Bruin, and E. Varèse in Eindhoven in the 1950s. As a solution for the dissociation between these two cultures, a "third culture"[185] suggests itself, but to this day this remains more of a dream than a reality.

5.3.2 Early and new music – the problem of mediated historical memory

So far, we have considered technology either as an inspirational factor or as a creative tool. In this chapter, we will instead try to put technology into the negative role of an inhibitor of the development of new music as a consequence of bringing older music into the present. The category of early or historical music was "discovered" in 1829, when Felix Mendelssohn-Bartholdy performed J. S. Bach's *Saint Matthew Passion* at the Sing-Akademie in Berlin. That act was important documentation of changing tastes consisting of the elevation of old ("dead") music to the level of contemporary ("living") music. From that moment onwards, the volume of early music existing alongside contemporary music began to increase gradually. The layers of sediment of music history from European culture were being archeologically rediscovered and brought to light, revived as part of a living culture, but this time in a different societal and historical context. Beginning in the 19th century, the attention of artists and the public was increasingly attracted not only by newly created music with a future orientation, but also by new discoveries reaching ever more deeply into music history.

---

185   Cf. SNOW, Charles Percy. *The Two Cultures*. Cambridge: Cambridge University Press, 1998.; BROCK-MAN, John. *The Third Culture: Beyond the Scientific Revolution*. Simon & Schuster, 1995; GIBODA, Michal (ed.). *Mosty a propasti mezi vědou a uměním*. České Budějovice: Dialog vědy s uměním v nakl. Tomáš Halama, 2010.

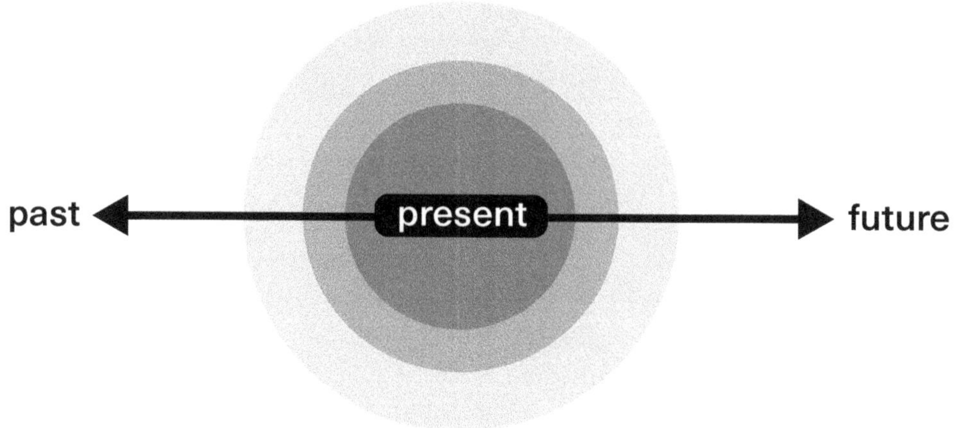

Fig. 12 Diagram of the growing volume of music currently being performed.

Another example of retrograde development was Stravinsky's unprecedented creative act in the form of his *Pulcinella*. Although Stravinsky was obviously using reminiscences of Baroque music, his critics were less than indulgent. Theodor Adorno, who used the phrase "music about music" in his *Philosophy of New Music*, wrote that Stravinsky was raping the music of our forefathers. He mainly criticised him for being servile to the authorities of early music.[186] Stravinsky made only a brief comment: *"Pulcinella was my discovery of the past, the epiphany through which the whole of my late work became possible. It was a backward look of course – the first of many love affairs in that direction – but it was a look in the mirror too."*[187]

By doing this, Stravinsky had by no means betrayed his position at the forefront of the interwar avant-garde. To the contrary, he again showed his originality, this time by the appropriation of a style, whereby he radically anticipated the postmodern polystylism of Alfred Schnittke by half a century. Stravinsky's abandonment of originality of style was very original in his day. At the same time, his idea of the relativity of progress in musical thinking is surprisingly classical (in the sense of adherence to the thinking of antiquity), but the idea is not unique in the 20th century. On the question of progress, Steve Reich commented:

"There's no such thing. That's hogwash! When you go from Gregorian chant to Machaut, you lose the suavity of one line. When you go from Gregorian chant to Perotin, you lose the beauty and refinement of one single line, and you gain these giant massive blocks of one tenor line and three decorative upper voices. When you move to Machaut, I actually find it kind of fussy, and kind of a let-down. The massiveness, the weight of Perotin is lost in the refinement, and the sort of hothouse environment, which was important to the

---

186   ADORNO, T. W. *Philosophie der Neuen Musik*. Frankfurt a. M.: Suhrkamp Verlag, 1976, p. 168.
187   Quoted by GARDNER, Howard. Igor Stravinsky: The Poetics and Politics of Music. *AVANT*, Vol. IV, No. 3/2013, p. 229.

Mannerists in the late fourteenth century. It's win some, lose some. When something is well done, it's well done. Whether it's a tune played on a solo flute or a massive orchestra and chorus is a descriptive situation, not a value judgment. Bigger isn't better, newer isn't better, older isn't better. Better is better, period. It would be so much easier if it were otherwise, but it isn't. [Laughs] We have to painfully examine each thing as it comes along, and there's no getting away from that."[188]

In this case, Stravinsky's originality meant the unmasking of the avant-garde's naïve faith in progress and the exposing of the cult of novelty that in itself fails to add value to music.

The issue raised by Mendelssohn-Bartholdy or Stravinsky is that of historical memory. They pointed out that whatever has not been forgotten (destroyed or lost) can at any time become a part of living culture and compete with the current products of musical thinking. Of course, historical memory is conditioned upon technology (i.e. media). Writing, musical notation, music printing, and later audio recordings are just different ways of encoding collective memory stored in various media. Today, thanks to recorded music, we are faced with the parallel existence of music of different historical periods as well as music of differing geographical and ethnic origin. Thanks to medialised musical memory, the space-time of musical culture has been compressed into a singularity.

In postmodern thinking, progress and linear development have been relativised. Today, we might almost say that the future has already passed by, and that music of the future is an anachronistic category.

There are two possible reasons for this paradoxical finding:

Firstly, early music has become an area of anticipated discoveries of the near future (i.e. newly discovered musical sources, new interpretations, the revival of specialised playing techniques on nearly forgotten instruments etc.). In terms of what is new, surprising, and unexpected, they offer the same thing as new music.

Secondly, in the latter half of the 20th century the concept of the new became outdated, even trite. We could hardly find anything more difficult and duller than the imperative of novelty, which Stravinsky simply replaced with the freedom of the old. Perhaps it was he who first recognised the importance of individual creative freedom, which absolutely cannot be limited by external circumstances, including the imperative of novelty.

Contemporary music does not live from the future. Forecasting the future belongs to the avant-gardes of the past. We look back into history and try to master the immense quantity of music composed in the past. Thanks to technologies, we have lost the ability to forget, which had always been a fundamental condition for new creation. Our collective memory, made permanent by every conceivable kind of media, makes it impossible for us to rid ourselves of the past. Moreover, the amount of new music being made seems negligible in comparison with the volume of existing

---

188   *Composer Steve Reich. Two Conversations with Bruce Duffie* [online]. [Accessed on 9 Oct. 2017]. Retrieved from: http://www.bruceduffie.com/reich.html.

music of various times and places, which is available to any one of us all the time. Contemporary music is thus necessarily condemned to confrontation with the music of the past. The result can be great uncertainty, the loss of the meaning of musical creation, or giving up on the ideas of progress and development.

The Italian Futurists, Arnold Schoenberg, John Cage, and others have become exhibits on display to predict the development of music, and today more than ever they remind us that the only thing in music that is given is its history. That history may or may not become a resource for present-day creation, while the future is a mere projection of our imaginings and desires.

5.3.3 The lonely author – a message in a bottle – the loss and transformation of the public

France was undoubtedly at the forefront of Europe-wide developments in the field of technologically conditioned music of the 20th century. The roots of French post-war techno-optimism reach back to the 1930s, when Henri de Saint-Simon and Charles Fourier formulated the utopian vision of a dialogue between artists, scientists, and engineers with artists in the main role in the investigation of reality.[189] As Hobsbawm[190] points out, the external forces influencing the arts in France after the Second World War were of a technological character because the country's economic boom was being driven by the progress taking place in the scientific and technical revolution. What we find in the early phases of the development of technologically conditioned music of the 20th century is a combination of advanced technology and primitive methods of working with sound often limited to an aleatoric approach or bricolage (J. Cage, P. Schaeffer etc.). Of interest in this context is Boulez's criticism of P. Schaeffer,[191] in which he asserted that efforts to gain control over technology had become an obsession with technology.[192] While new events in the field of electroacoustic music were causing literal sensations and scandals in the early 1950s, by the end of the 1960s that current of music had become something routine incorporated into both art music and popular music. Already in earlier studies,[193] we have referred to Dahlhaus's comment that by around 1970, electroacoustic music had lost its attraction, both negative and positive, and had become a routine phenomenon.

---

189 TAYLOR, Timothy D. *Strange Sounds: Music, Technology and Culture*. NY, London: Routledge, 2001. Cf. BORN, Georgina. *Rationalizing Culture: IRCAM, Boulez and the Institutionalization of the Musical Avant-Garde*. Berkeley and Los Angeles: University of California Press, 1995, p. 71.

190 HOBSBAWM, Eric. *The Age of Extremes: A History of the World, 1914–1991*, p. 501. Cit. in TAYLOR, op. cit., p. 44.

191 In BOULEZ, Pierre. Concrete (Music). In *Notes of an Apprenticeship*. A. A. Knopf, 1968, pp. 289–290.

192 Cf. TAYLOR, op. cit., pp. 55–57.

193 Cf. in particular Der Osten des Westens: Elektroakustische Musik in der Tschechoslowakei von 1948 bis 1992. In *Sound Exchange: Experimentelle Musikkulturen in Mitteleuropa*. Saarbrücken: PFAU Verlag, 2012, pp. 172–181.

"Die elektronische Musik hat ihre Schrecken verloren, zugleich aber auch die passionierte Teilnahme, der sie in den ersten Jahren begegnete. Sie ist, nachdem si zunächst von einer aufgestörten Publizistik ins Zentrum der Neuen Musik gerückt worden war, zu einem Randphänommen verblasst."[194]

The musicologist's comment is affirmed by a statement made by the composer Luciano Berio.[195] In 1976, he noticed that as the years went by, it was becoming harder to find musicians and journalists maintaining the optimistic and futuristic mood of the 1950s. He compared works of electroacoustic music to a message in a bottle tossed into the sea—not many people manage to receive and understand it. He wrote that it is difficult even to define the term electronic [sic] music; it can be defined neither by the use of technical resources nor through general principles common to other forms of musical thought. He made the paradoxical comment that in a certain sense, electronic music no longer actually exists because it is everywhere and is part of contemporary musical thinking. "*La musica elettronica in un certo senso 'non esiste' più perché è dappertutto e fa parte del pensare musicale di tutti i giorni.*"[196] We can describe its specific techniques, but we cannot define it as an antithesis with respect to other methods and conceptions of musical creation. According to Berio, however, knowledge of electroacoustic music is of key importance for every composer for the very reason that it is so widespread. In short, it is becoming a necessary part of education that cannot be ignored.

The subject matter of this chapter is analysis of various kinds of increasing criticism and scepticism of technologically conditioned music from the 1950s onwards. Criticism of electroacoustic music should help us discover and understand the motivations for and causes of the rejection of electronic technology as a mechanism for rescuing New Music, which found itself in a similar crisis during the same period. At the same time, we must pose a question that can function here as a hypothesis: "Are the changes to the development of music being initiated by far more general trends, such as, for example, the questioning of the modern conception of technological progress and innovation?" Another circumstance that might lead one to believe that electroacoustic music is losing its public is the fact that the cost of electronic musical technologies has been constantly declining, making the instruments widely available. For this reason, part of the public spills over into the field of musical creation, becoming creators instead of listeners. This hypothesis is supported by the fact that no later than by the 1970s, popular musical genres (jazz, rock, and pop) were undergoing rapid development with electronic technologies playing a leading role. This democratisation of technologies causes a mass exodus of listeners and fans from concerts of electroacoustic art music towards creative

---

194　DAHLHAUS, Carl. Ästhetische Probleme der elektronischen Musik. In *Experimentelle Musik: Schriftenreihe der Akademie der Künste*. Band 7. Berlin: Gebr. Mann Verlag, 1970, p. 81.

195　BERIO, Luciano. Prefazione. In *La musica elettronica: Testi scelti e commentati da Henri Pousseur*. Milano: Feltrinelli Editore, p. vii.

196　Ibid.

work of their own. This idea is also supported by some statements made by popular musicians who claim Karlheinz Stockhausen, for example, as a role model (Beatles, Björk, Aphex Twin etc.). The German band Kraftwerk (founded in 1970) commented:

> "[The idea was] to be in a real dialogue and listen to the wonders of technology in the way that natural laws are applied in the music – the physical laws of music and sound in combination with artistic ideas – and not just ignore everything. Our idea was really this combination of men and machines, and for us, it has worked very well. [...] ours is the creative side of machines, making music with pocket calculators and computers and creating interesting images and art forms. That's the main essence of what it's all about and has been since Bach did the 'Well Tempered Piano' at a time when the piano was the latest invention."[197]

The Icelandic musician Björk mentions Stockhausen in describing her motivations:

> "I remember being almost the fighter in the school, the odd kid out, with a real passion for music, but against all this retro, constant Beethoven and Bach bollocks. Most of it was this frustration with the school's obsession with the past. When I was introduced to Stockhausen it was like 'aaah'! Finally somebody was speaking my language. Stockhausen has said phrases like, 'We should listen to 'old' music one day a year and the other 364 days we should listen to 'now' music. And we should do it in the same way as we look through photo albums of when we were children. If you look at old photo albums too often they just become pointless. You start indulging in something that doesn't matter, and you stop worrying about the present.' And that's how he looked at all those people who are obsessed with old music. For a kid born of my generation who was 12 at that time it was brilliant, because at the same time I was also being introduced to the electronic music of bands like Kraftwerk and DAF."[198]

It seems that the loss or transformation of the New Music public is a problem with roots reaching back to sometime around the 19th century. This is not just a problem of musical reception and consumption, but also of production. The loss of the public can be both the cause and the effect of problems with new musical creation. If we proceed from the assumption that shared culture, i.e. culture that takes place in the "here and now" in a single spatiotemporal framework of production and reception, has the highest degree of authenticity,[199] the fragmentation of that framework must necessarily generate inauthentic, mediated communication

---

197   HARRINGTON, Richard. These Days, Kraftwerk Is Packing Light. *The Washington Post.* May 27, 2005. Retrieved from: https://www.washingtonpost.com/archive/lifestyle/2005/05/27/these-days-kraftwerk-is-packing-light/300d99ad-29df-4f42-8270-0cc61eafa3b7/.

198   BJÖRK. *Compose Yourself: Entretien Björk & Karlheinz Stockhausen.* Dazed & Confused, n°23, août 1996, pp. 42–46 [online]. [Accessed on 19 June 2023]. Retrieved from: https://www.bjork.fr/Dazed-Confused-no23.

199   Cf. SCRUTON, Roger. *An Intelligent Person's Guide to Modern Culture.* London: Duckworth, 1998.

shaping a different cultural experience. Simon Emmerson has investigated what role new technologies can play in this in his book *Living Electronic Music*.[200] He writes that electronic technologies have led to three great "acousmatic dislocations", meaning the separation of the public from the originator of the sound or music. The first is temporal dislocation, caused by the arrival of audio recordings beginning with the phonogram in 1877. The second is spatial dislocation imposed by the arrival of recordings, telecommunications, and radio, and the third is mechanical dislocation that puts machines in place of humans in the causative role (recordings, electronic synthesis, telecommunications).[201] These causes of dislocation are not mutually exclusive; they are accumulative. Thanks to the loss of ties to these kinds of causality, composers are losing the possibility of communicating with their public. Taylor has commented similarly on this problem, noting that while electroacoustic music can now be produced live, it usually is not. Everyone sits in their studios or at their computers in private—music is no longer a social experience.[202]

Can one agree with this explanation unconditionally? For example, is a novel a regression from oral storytelling? Is an e-book a disruption of communication between the storyteller and the listener? This explanation is not satisfactory. We could object that despite the complicated technological chain that exists between the author and the recipient of a work, e-books have served to increase interest in old forms like the novel or novella. The same also applies to LP records, films, magnetic tapes, CDs, MP3s, or streaming portals, which have repeatedly stimulated new interest in old cultural forms. It is just the methods, interfaces, and media of communication that are changing.

5.3.4 The question of the authenticity of technological music

The problem of aesthetic authenticity of technologically conditioned music can also be appropriately demonstrated using the history of computer and game music.[203] Paradoxically, it turns out that there are two contradictory tendencies in the development of game music: one that is technologically innovative and a second one that is stylistically regressive. While the development of hardware technologies for creating and processing music is moving forwards, the aesthetic models of game music are either stagnant or are actually going back to the roots of the medium, which are in film. Hollywood films with their post-Romantic symphonic music are thus becoming the models for the mainstream production of game music. From the beginning of game music's existence, Hollywood film music has been its aesthetic ideal, and it just

---

200 Ashgate, 2007.

201 EMMERSON, op. cit., p. 91.

202 TAYLOR, op. cit., p. 139.

203 Cf. FLAŠAR, Martin. The Hollywood Sound Paradox: A Regress of Game Music to Film Music Origins. *Hudba - Integrácie - Interpretácie*. Nitra: Univerzita Konštantína Filozófa v Nitre, 2017, Vol. 20, No. 1, pp. 247–273.

took a few decades for computer hardware and memory capacity to make it possible to include such music in games. Here, I shall take the liberty of quoting my own text:

> "As we can observe, game music since its early beginnings used to bear distinctive imprints of the medium. Its variety was indisputably limited by both hardware and software conditions. Thus, music and sound displayed or mirrored the possibilities of the used media. In terms of aesthetics this type of music can be perceived as having a high rate of authenticity. The mastery of overcoming the new technical limitations was comparable to a mastery of a classical music composer dealing with physical givens of the traditional music instrument.
>
> [...]
>
> What we have been witnessing in recent years is a slow but obvious disappearance of authenticity of technologically produced game music. Whereas the first videogames used native sounds produced by rather technically poor chips and in that way represented an authentic product of contemporary hardware (i.e. musical instrument), later, following the growing potential of the hardware, the sounds produced by it became increasingly artificial, virtual and estranged to its hardware source. The first authors and music makers perhaps dreamt about the sounds of the violin, the piano or the human voice, but during the hunt for perfect simulation of traditional musical instruments nobody realized the loss of something incomparably more valuable, namely the authenticity of real digital instruments."[204]

Technologically conditioned music can be regarded as authentic if it is aesthetically relevant for its use of hardware resources. The musical instrument of software is hardware, and not the simulation of real acoustical instruments. According to this premise, authentic computer music would be software-generated music, the possibilities of which are limited by the hardware. In other words, in the environment of new technologies, there does not exist any objective conditionality of simulation of old instruments. Here, the limits are the possibilities of the electronics and basic mathematical and physical processes. At the highest level of abstraction, a system of equations can become, in a certain sense, a musical instrument, as Milan Guštar has remarked.[205]

The orientation of the aesthetic of a large part of computer music and electroacoustic music towards the simulation of older instruments and forms may be a consequence of disappointment over the unfulfilled techno-optimism of the 1950s and '60s. The result has been various kinds of technological or aesthetic nostalgia, such as the recycling of the unique, provisional aesthetics of the sound of 8-bit computers, as in the cases of the musical styles bitcore, bithop, bliphop, chiptunes, or micromusic.[206]

---

204 Ibid., pp. 248–250.

205 Cf. FLAŠAR, Martin. Hudebním nástrojem může být dnes soustava rovnic... In VOJTĚCHOVSKÝ, Miloš. *Milan Guštar*. Praha: DOX Prague, 2013, pp. 99–102.

206 Cf. FLAŠAR, Martin. *Elektroakustická hudba* [online]. 1st edition. Brno: Masarykova univerzita, 2015. [Accessed on 6 Feb. 2018]. Elportál. Retrieved from: http://is.muni.cz/elportal/?id=1308636.

5.4 Post-technological solutions for music

The rejection of technology can take a whole range of forms. Post-technological departure points in music are not so much an attitude opposed to technology, as in the case of techno-scepticism, but instead a stance informed by technologies. Post-technological solutions for music are influenced by technological developments, but they dismiss technology as something expendable because what is important is the aesthetic result to which the use of technology has led. Post-technological stances arise at the moment when faith in technology as the main means of music's revitalisation or innovation has been overcome. Most of these strategies did not arrive until after the heyday of musical technologies, which we may regard as the 20-year period from around the end of the 1940s until the beginning of the 1970s, but there were even some composers who raised critical voices, doubting the importance of the new technologies at the time of their greatest flourishing (e.g. György Ligeti). There were also those who hesitantly vacillated for a long time between live acoustic music and electroacoustic music and involved themselves in both worlds in parallel (e.g. Karlheinz Stockhausen or Iannis Xenakis).

The following subchapters represent four characteristic post-technological stances that we have identified with composers and artists at the turn of the 20th and 21st centuries:

1. Criticism of technology – this arrives with the rise of Postmodernism, which calls technology into question as a tool of progress and of development through innovation, as a tool for the creation of things of permanent value, or as a tool for musical communication of greater quality. The group of approaches in this subchapter understand electronic technology as a negative phenomenon that should be eliminated.
2. Adaptation of technological models in live acoustic music – this shows the possibilities for overcoming electronic technology in music by a positive approach to technologies. Certain composers take technologically created models as their departure point and adapt them for the conditions of purely "human" music. They transcribe models manually into scores that are interpreted by live performers.
3. Recycling of technology – this positive strategy strives to use discarded electronic technologies for new audio or musical purposes. The emphasis is on sustainable solutions, creativity, playfulness, and unpredictability.
4. Inspiration by technology – this positive group exemplifies post-technological approaches to musical production that are based on the aesthetic changes brought about by electronic technologies without necessarily continuing to be dependent upon them.

5.4.1 Criticism of technology

5.4.1.1 Does postmodern equal post-technological?

The technological exhaustion that arrived in the 1970s was the exhaustion of the modern analogue, basically mechanical (industrial) era. That state of affairs overlaps with the arrival of Postmodernism in philosophy and the arts, which evaluates technology from its own perspective. Postmodernism does not reject technology as a product of the modern era in general, but it refuses to view it as an instrument of progress and dominance.

> "'Progress', once the most extreme manifestation of radical optimism and a promise of universally shared and lasting happiness, has moved all the way to the opposite, dystopian and fatalistic pole of anticipation: it now stands for the threat of a relentless and inescapable change that instead of auguring peace and respite portends nothing but continuous crisis and strain and forbids a moment of rest. [...] Instead of great expectations and sweet dreams, 'progress' evokes an insomnia full of nightmares of 'being left behind' [...]."[207]

Lyotard also warns against humanity's inability to keep pace with the tempo of technological changes and the process of accumulation of new objects of theory and practice.[208] From a mere resource, technology has become an imperative or a threat. Society's reaction is resignation and anxiety over its own insufficiency, which can simply lead to the abandonment of technology. The progress of technology is no longer human progress because it is not based on human needs, but rather on the needs of technology itself.[209] The subject driving changes is therefore not mankind, but instead the technology itself. On the basis of newly emerging technologies, the need for society to have this technology at its disposal is then retroactively, artificially induced.

The relationship between technological development and music in the era of Postmodernism represents a special problem. As Vít Zouhar has pointed out, the word "postmodern" does not appear before 1980 in musicological discourse, while in literature studies we already find it in 1969 (Leslie Fiedler), in architecture in 1975 (Charles Jencks), and in philosophy in 1979 (Jean-François Lyotard).[210]

Historically, the first herald of Postmodernism in musicology is Wulf Konold in his lecture published later as *Komponieren in der „Postmoderne"* (1980).[211] He regards the following conditions as the key to composing in the postmodern era:

---

207   BAUMAN, Zygmunt. *Liquid Times: Living in an Age of Uncertainty.* Cambridge: Polity Press, 2007, pp. 10–11.

208   LYOTARD, Jean-François. *The Postmodern Explained to Children: Correspondence, 1982–1985.* Turnaround, 1992, pp. 91–92.

209   Ibid.

210   ZOUHAR, Vít. *Postmoderní hudba?: německá diskuse na sklonku 20. století.* Olomouc: Univerzita Palackého v Olomouci, 2004. Monografie, pp. 14–16.

211   KONOLD, Wulf. Komponieren in der „Postmoderne". In *Hindemith Jahrbuch,* 1981, H. 10, p. 83, cit. in ZOUHAR, op. cit., p. 79.

— an avoidance of experimentation,
— distrust of the new,
— an inclination towards the institutionalisation of the arts,
— interest in the listener,
— escape from reality, characterised by regionalisation, the cult of harmony, and ties to tradition.[212]

If we understand technological development as a condition for experimental music or as a synonym for the "new", this contradicts Konold's definition of the basic framework of musical Postmodernism. Postmodernism does not believe in progress realised through technology even in music.

The technological exhaustion apparent in the 1970s was not resolved until the arrival of the popular culture of new media represented mainly by the personal computers of the 1980s like the Atari, Commodore Amiga, and Apple McIntosh, MIDI (1983), General MIDI (1991), and the arrival of the first digital synthesizer, the Yamaha DX-7 (1983). The democratisation of new multimedia technologies and the relative simplicity of their operation made them powerful tools in the hands of a large base of users and of musicians who were not particularly technologically skilled. Paradoxically, this has led to a schizophrenic situation: the line of development of musical technologies begun by Modernism continues, yet it has alienated a considerable part of society, thought, and culture, which view it critically.

5.4.1.2 The music of today as the trash of tomorrow. Liquidity vs. stability of resources

Another risk factor causing scepticism in the musical implementation of the results of technological progress is the dynamic rate of that technological progress. Gérard Grisey, a leading representative of French electroacoustic music, discussed the difficulty of cultural integration of technological resources during precipitous developments. In an interview for the journal *20th-Century Music* in March 1996, he had this to say about his relationship with technology:[213]

"Technology forces me to go back and work over again. A new tape. Changing from a tape to computer. And then from computer to a new type of computer. Or from one synthesizer to a new type. And it's endless. [I suppose there will come a time when] things are going to be stabilized. Well, I hope. But you know, a few years ago we all thought the Yamaha DX-7, for instance, was going to be stabilized. A lot of composers have written pieces for this wonderful instrument, and I have done it, too – integrating it in a large orchestra. Here we are with an instrument that is already totally outdated, and it's going to be hard to find one in a few years. We belong to a throw-away society,

---

212 Ibid., pp. 87–88.
213 GRISEY, Gérard. *Gerard Grisey, an Interview* [online]. [Accessed on 10 April 2018]. Retrieved from: http://www.angelfire.com/music2/davidbundler/grisey.html.

you see, so they ask for pieces that are not supposed to last more than a few years. I don't want to be part of that."[214]

Here, Grisey is dealing with the problem of the rapid development of technologies, which prevent the stabilisation of individual instruments in cultural development, as the instruments become superseded by one new form after another. This situation resists the arising of virtuosity as the supreme ability to make use of a given instrument's technical potential. Let us take as an example the traditional musical instruments found in a symphony orchestra. The oldest of them have been around for several centuries and have remained basically unchanged for hundreds of years. A stable instrument with structural development that is finished (at least in basic principle) allows the long-term creation of repertoire, the development of new playing techniques, and the associated didactics for playing the instrument. In this way, over time every instrument builds a sphere within musical culture, a musical subculture for the instrument in question. The impact of technology is therefore directly socio-institutional, creating interest groups surrounding the given instrument. The speed and liquidity of development and changes in the latter half of the 20th century and afterwards limit the creation of such subcultures. The result of this dynamic is the liquidation of potential social groups that would advance the potential of the given instrument. This leads to quick solutions, eruptions of interest in new technologies, and subsequently an equally rapid cooling of interest in them and their abandonment.

Zygmunt Bauman addresses the question of the liquidity, dynamic changeability, and ephemerality of the present-day arts in connection with his concept of liquid modernity. In the study *Liquid Arts*,[215] he devotes himself to the transformations of societal and aesthetic values in the period of Postmodernism. As he points out, consumer society of the early 21st century is not characterised by the obtaining and accumulation of things, but rather by their consumption (disposal) and replacement with new things.

> "Liquid modern life is a daily rehearsal of universal transience. Today's useful and indispensable objects, with few and possibly no exceptions, are tomorrow's waste. Everything is disposable, nothing is truly necessary, nothing is irreplaceable. Everything is born engraved with the brand of death. Everything is offered with a use-by date attached."[216]

Bauman applies this premise not only to things, but also to people (who are consumed in interpersonal relationships or on television shows) and to culture and the arts, of course. Bauman turns his attention to the aesthetic question of the beautiful and asserts that the beautiful has historically always been associated with the perfect (i.e. that which is complete). Although philosophers have never agreed about the

---

214   Ibid.

215   *Theory Culture & Society*, 2007, 24, pp. 117–126.

216   Ibid., pp. 123–124.

general characteristics of the arts, they have agreed with each other that the arts are not ephemeral, but permanent, long lasting or, ideally, immortal, with a tendency towards universal validity. Bauman explicitly highlights these two characteristics of the arts: timelessness and universality. In keeping with Alberti's definition of perfection (and contrary to Umberto Eco's theory of the open artwork), he asserts that while art is the child of changes and development, the achieving of perfection means the elimination of the need for any more changes, which could only be for the worse. Achieving perfection means the end of all changes. Given the present state of society, completeness and perfection mean a nightmare according to Bauman because completeness represents stagnation, the end of development and movement, and the end of adventure. Therefore, according to Bauman, we are living in a world filled with aesthetic objects but not with art.

5.4.1.3 Postmusic?

For some theoreticians, the situation with contemporary music is extremely dismal. In 2008, Jody Berland, a Canadian expert on the relationship between music and technology, came up with the term "postmusic", even using it in the plural (postmusics).[217] It is necessary to free oneself of the attractive rhetoric of the confusing postmodern, post-humanist, post-digital, and post-internet era and to give the arguments of this theory a critical examination. Her point of departure is Attali's comment that today's contemporary composers are scarcely anything more than people who listen to music they have created on their own computers.[218] This means that music is undergoing a process of disembodiment, in which bodily contact with an instrument does not occur. She writes:

> "You do not need guitar or piano lessons; you do not need to practise every day. If listeners appear they are not sitting in judgement of you. You do not have to know how to move your hands, sing in tune, count with your breath or vibrate an object with your body. You just have to study your manual, watch the screen, listen, choose and press enter."[219]

If we enumerate the basic features of what the author calls "postmusic", we get the following list:

1. absence of colleagues – individual creation (communication by network),
2. absence of an audience – the music is recorded in a studio imitating a live recording, which in turn imitates a live concert,

---

217 BERLAND, Jody. Postmusics. In Gerry Bloustien, Margaret Peters and Susan Luckman (eds.). *Sonic Synergies: Music, Technology, Community, Identity*. Ashgate Publishing Ltd.: Hampshire, 2008, pp. 27–37.

218 ATTALI, Jacques. *Noise: the political economy of music*. Minneapolis: University of Minnesota Press, 1985, p. 115.

219 BERLAND, op. cit., pp. 36–37.

3. absence of a musical performance – the recording is better,
4. absence of hearing – the music is manipulated exclusively in the form of a visual representation,
5. absence of instruments – the music is not made by playing musical instruments, but by the playing of machines (*musicking machine*).
6. absence of rehearsals – during recording, the performer is not responsible for the result of the recording (a technician is responsible). The subject is merely the subject of the recording.

This list clearly shows what the author has in mind by the term "postmusic": the actual absence of all the basic parts of the traditional communication (production-reception) model that in aggregate we call music. This does not involve the negation of music as such, but the replacement by impersonal machines of the part of the model that had been assigned exclusively to human experience. The collective, live experience of musical production is replaced by a studio recording in which machines intended for the production and processing of sound play in increasingly important role.

5.4.1.4 Petr Nikl: Technological ecology

Petr Nikl has presented one of the possible solutions for the arts of our time. He conceives his expositions as an open environment encouraging interactive playing.[220] He calls his reaction to the period of excessive faith in electronic technology "technological ecology". Nikl employed his post-technological artistic approach to create the Czech exhibit *Garden of Fantasy and Music* at EXPO 2005 in Aichi, Japan.

His collaborative audiovisual interactive installation was prepared with Petr Lorenc, Milan Cais, Ondřej Smeykal, Martin Janíček, Jaroslav Kořán, and Václav Smolka. Like in his other exhibitions and artistic realisations, he does entirely without electronic technologies, using only the basic laws of mechanics and natural phenomena. Although Nikl is also an active musician and author, in this case he merely conceived the external conditions for musical play by the visitors. About the strategy of his exhibit, he commented:

"It is an effort to set up some kind of alternative to the sphere of the computer, a kind of technological ecology. We are getting back to nature by filling the space with instruments that function on basic optical and acoustical principles."[221]

---

220 Concerning the idea of play in culture, cf. HUIZINGA, Johan. *Homo Ludens*, op. cit. and GADAMER, Hans-Georg. *The Relevance of the Beautiful and Other Essays*, op. cit.

221 MF DNES, aho. *Češi na Expo: říše plná hudby a fantazie* [online]. 25 March 2005, 9:28. Retrieved from: http://kultura.zpravy.idnes.cz/cesi-na-expo-rise-plna-hudby-a-fantazie-dhc-/vytvarne-umeni.aspx?c=2005M071a10B.

Fig. 13 a–b *Garden of Fantasy and Music*. EXPO 2005, Aichi. Petr Nikl created the interactive exhibition's concept. Artists participating in the exhibition: Petr Lorenc, Milan Cais, Ondřej Smeykal, Martin Janíček, Jaroslav Kořán, and Václav Smolka. Source: Archive of Petr Nikl.

The key terms for Nikl's creative aesthetics are play, nature, fantasy, and fiction. He creates fictional worlds that invite people to interact with material, achieving complex effects by simple means, and everything that matters takes place at the level of individual imagination. The basic characteristic of his exhibitions is the mediation of simple causality between visitors' actions and the reactions of the instruments, thereby restoring people's comprehension of the process of making music through the joy of playing.

5.4.2 Adaptation of technological models in composed music

The solution to Heidegger's theoretical proposal for mankind's "spiritual" coming to terms with technology appears in music almost immediately after it was formulated. It was as if the need for humanisation of technology, i.e. its harnessing to the creative process, was the generally accepted current task of the post-war decades. In the three following cases, we attempt the inductive description of a strategy that we call the adaptation of technological models in live or acoustically composed music. This involves four selected types of technological working models: additive synthesis, looping, phase shifting, and remixing. The strategy of internalising or adopting originally technologically produced models is a practical reaction of composers to the need for humanising technology.

5.4.2.1 György Ligeti: Adoption of the model of additive synthesis

Ligeti left Hungary in 1956 and settled in Vienna. He was then invited by Herbert Eimert to the WDR studio in Cologne, where in 1957–58 he engaged in intensive study of the music of Karlheinz Stockhausen, Mauricio Kagel, and Pierre Boulez. His work at the studio resulted in a few compositions: *Glissandi* (1957), the unfinished *Pièce électronique Nr. 3* (1957), and *Artikulation* (1958), which attracted the attention of experts.[222] As Jennifer Iverson has pointed out,[223] it was thanks to Ligeti's experience with electroacoustic music that he discovered a technique for working with timbre that he applied directly in his purely acoustic micropolyphony. This involved a style of working with sound masses (of a different kind from those used by Xenakis), which was reflected in his orchestral works *Apparitions* (1958–1959) and *Atmosphères* (1961). Symptomatically, Ligeti abandoned electroacoustic music definitively, which he justified on the grounds of dissatisfaction with the sounds he could achieve by electronic manipulation. Ligeti's rejection therefore was not because of the level of quality of available technology, but because of aesthetically unsatisfactory results.

---

222 *György Ligeti* [online]. [Accessed on 5 Sept. 2018]. Retrieved from: http://www.schott-music.com/shop/persons/featured/gyoergy-ligeti.

223 IVERSON, Jennifer. The Emergence of Timbre: Ligeti's Synthesis of Electronic and Acoustic Music in Atmosphères. *Twentieth-Century Music*, 2010, 7, pp. 61–89.

"Ich befinde mich in den letzten Jahren in einem Zustand, in dem ich ein wenig unbefriedigt bin über die akustischen Ergebnisse dessen, was man im elektronischen Studio machen kann, unabhängig davon, welche Studioeinrichtung vorhanden ist, es geht nicht um die Perfektion der Studioeinrichtung."[224]

Pièce électronique Nr. 3 remained unfinished for technical reasons because the studio's equipment did not make it possible to work with 48 independent voices. After leaving the studio and, by extension, the world of electroacoustic music behind, Ligeti retained the central position of timbre in his aesthetic, but he adapted the method of additive synthesis (the addition and layering of sound waves) to music that is performed live. Unlike in simple additive synthesis, however, every voice of his *Atmosphères* represents the entire spectrum of harmonics. The adaptation of the model of additive synthesis to acoustic music that is performed live was one of the key examples of both the use and the surpassing of electronic technologies in music.

5.4.2.2 Steve Reich: Adaptation of the model of looping and phase shifting

Other examples of the adapting of a model created technologically for compositions to be performed live are looping and phase shifting. Although the principle of looping (repetition) is obviously as old as music itself, in European art music we routinely find two-fold (repeat signs or the exposition and recapitulation of sonata form etc.) or even three-fold (e.g. A. Vivaldi's sequences or at least three occurrences of the refrain in a rondo) repetitions. Eric Satie finally explored the effect of extreme repetition on the perception of musical structure in the case of his *Vexations* (1893) for piano, which is supposed to be repeated 840 times. An extreme number of repetitions leads to the listener's loss of concentration on the musical motif as an object (a "figure" according to Gestalt psychology), leading to the shifting of its perception to the "background". This principle is plentifully employed by American repetitive (or ostinato) minimalism, which shifts the emphasis from intentional, "objective" perception of music to subconscious experience against the background of a repeating musical structure.[225] The first example of this is the American composer Steve Reich (*1936). The character of his creative aesthetics was defined in the 1960s by experiments with audio tape loops. The music he has composed is the direct result of practical technological experiments with that medium. At first, this involved experiments with human speech in loops. That is how he composed *It's Gonna Rain* (1965) and *Come Out* (1966). He also wrote a series of compositions titled *Phases* for various instruments using the principle of phase shifting. They were based on

---

224 LIGETI, György. *Auswirkungen der elektronischen Musik*, GS, Vol. 2, p. 77. Cit. in IVERSON, op. cit., 2010, p. 62, footnote no. 9.

225 For more on this subject: FLAŠAR, Martin. Minimal music jako problém figury a pozadí. In RUSINO-VÁ, Zora and KRALOVIČ, Ján. *Serialita a repetícia: Zborník z Mezinárodného interdisciplinárneho sympózia*. Bratislava: Katedra teórie a dejín umenia, Vysoká škola výtvarných umení v Bratislave, 2017, pp. 64–71.

experiments with two tape players, with the author manually slowing down the reel on one of the machines during playback.

Reich's classic *Different Trains* (1988)[226] is written for string quartet and tape, on which are recorded three more string quartets, spoken comments (analogous to the speech melodies of Leoš Janáček), and other sound samples. Reich's sound manipulation reached its climax in his documentary video-opera *Three Tales* (2001), combining techniques of electroacoustic music (loops, slow-motion sound, stop-motion sound, phase shift etc.) with compositional techniques of traditional acoustic material.

5.4.2.3 Martin Smolka: Adaptation of remixing

In 2000, Martin Smolka was commissioned by Musica Viva München to compose a 16-minute work for large orchestra titled *Remix, Redream, Reflight*. Although the composer uses the word "remix" in the title, that word is usually used for working with a sound recording rather than with musical notation. This is therefore an adaptation of a technique and term for the practice of composing music to be played live. The more accurate term would be "recomposition" because the work involves the deconstruction of the original musical structure, the excerpting of chords as objects, and using them in a new context. In the first half of the work, the composer recycles objects excerpted from music by Beethoven, Berlioz, Franck, Kabeláč, Tchaikovsky, and Mahler. From a sequence of secco chords (four minor chords, one major sixth chord, and one minor-major seventh chord) he creates a loop that is gradually shortened.[227] The composer draws more material from three sequences of mostly continuous chords from Mozart's *Symphony No. 41 in C major, K. 551*, Beethoven's *Wind Octet in E flat major, Op. 103*, and the Adagietto of Mahler's *Symphony No. 5 in C sharp minor*. The chords from the various pieces appear in alternation, and they are further Developed by the successive dropping out of chord tones (instrumental parts). Instead of variations, the music is gradually permeated by new elements in the freely fanciful style of music of the late 20th century.

Smolka explains the initial inspiration for his composition as follows:

> "At the Ježek Conservatoire I attended a thorough lecture about contemporary dance music created on computers using all possible kinds of stylistic genres and technical equipment. As I understood it, a creative DJ has in his computer a lot of rock, pop, jazz, and whatever other kinds of music broken down into their components. From those components, he composes a collage. I was especially fascinated by equipment that simply plays, and the creator proceeds by taking things away. On the way back home, I enjoyed imagining what classical music reprocessed using this technique would be like. In my mind, I glued together in loops the final chords of Classical and Romantic symphonies,

---

226   Cf. chapter 5.1.

227   *Remix, Redream, Reflight* (2000) [online]. [Accessed on 5 Mar. 2018]. Retrieved from: http://www.martinsmolka.com/works/remix.html.

Fig. 14 M. Smolka: *Remix, Redream, Reflight* (2000), bars 270-274.
Source: http://www.martinsmolka.com/scores/remixsc.html.

and in place of techno beats, the music was played by typical percussion of the 19th century—bass drum, triangle, and crash cymbals."[228]

This raises the question: How do you remain a contemporary composer and not write new music? The solution is to recontextualise old music into a new musical structure. If we set aside the technological aspect, what we have here is the standard answer of the post-modern composer, who confronts ubiquitous musical-cultural memory by using the method of sampling.

---

228   Ibid.

5.4.3 Recycling of technology

5.4.3.1 Nicolas Collins: hardware hacking as a strategy of live electronic music

> "We live in a cut and paste world: Control-X and Control-V give us the freedom to rearrange words, pictures, video and sound to transform any old thing into our new thing with tremendous ease and power. But, by and large, this is also an 'off-line' world, whose digital tools, as powerful as they might be, are more suitable to preparing texts, photo albums, movies and CDs in private, rather than on stage. These days most 'live electronic music' seems to be hibernating, its tranquil countenance only disturbed from time to time by the occasional, discrete click of a mouse."
>
> Nicolas Collins: *Hardware Hacking*[229]

Nicolas Collins has noticed that artists producing music on their laptop computers are indistinguishable from someone answering e-mails with music playing in the background.[230] He refers to Miller Puckette, creator of the programming language for Pure Data interactive multimedia, who clearly says that for the public, there must be a direct, comprehensible relationship between the actions of the performer (or the musical instrument or interface being used) and the sounds we are hearing. A performer pressing a button and activating a corresponding process gives us no information about how the music is really created. We learn everything important on the basis of hearing. Once again, computer music and generative music bring back into play the old problem of acousmatic music intended exclusively for listening. As we have attempted to show in chapter 4, the experience is unnatural and unusual for listeners. People do not routinely find themselves in situations where they must rely strictly on their sense of hearing. Sound that is not visibly produced by a physical action is an unprecedented system of signs, like Baudrillard's map without a territory or a simulacrum without a preceding reality.[231]

At the same time, a computer is a relatively complicated medium, which stands between the artist and the resulting sound artefact. The departure point for Nick Collins's essential discussion of electroacoustic music that is produced live[232] is the assertion that computer music does not represent real "live electronic music". It is more reminiscent of quiet work in a laboratory than of a live production on stage, and we can only speculate about its immediacy in performance. According to Collins, computers are wonderful things, but their ordinary interface and their ASCII keyboard and mouse make their use a relatively mediated activity in performance. Live music should be made with the musician and the sound in direct

---

229 COLLINS, Nicolas. *Hardware Hacking*. Rev. 2.1, May 2004, p. 4.

230 COLLINS, Nicolas. Generative Music and Laptop Performance. *Contemporary Music Review*, 2003, Vol. 22, No. 4, p. 67.

231 For more on the question of musical simulacra, see CSERES, Jozef. *Hudobné simulakrá*. Bratislava: Hudobné centrum, 2001.

232 COLLINS, Nicolas. *Hardware Hacking*, op. cit.

contact in a process of the immediate, physical manipulation of sound. He therefore emphasises the creation of instruments intended for live playing, aids for recording, and instruments making unusual sounds. His DIY (*do-it-yourself*) strategy is based on the physical manipulation (*hacking*) of hardware for the purpose of finding new sounds and creating situations whereby unusual combinations of uses of electronic components produce new sound outputs. The author, an inventor of sounds, is not facing a prefabricated configuration of commercially available instruments (as in the case of synthesizers), but instead becomes the manipulator of possibilities that the electronics offer.

5.4.3.2 John Richards: Composition of post-optimal objects

> "Death by a thousand music apps: a sampler, favourite virtual synth or mobile studio. Music technology brought to the fingertips. Record in hi-resolution any time, any place, anywhere. No limits! But to what musical ends? It is not necessarily a question of being anti-technology, a kind of digital Romanticism, but thinking post-optimal towards a more critical use of and relationship with technology."
>
> John Richards: *Slippery Bows and Slow Circuits*[233]

John Richards offers a similar solution to the problem of the dematerialisation of the process of music generation. The poetics of this English composer and introducer of DIY electronic instruments are based on the recycling of *post-optimal electronic objects*. Richards has borrowed this term from Anthony Dunne,[234] who suggests a shift of the function of electronic equipment from practical towards poetic use, into the area of philosophy, poetry, and aesthetics. Like Heidegger in the 1950s, Dunne believes that the solution of the technology problem is not to disavow technology, but to turn to it poetically. Let us recall Heidegger's proposal:

> "Because the essence of technology is nothing technological, essential reflection upon technology and decisive confrontation with it must happen in a realm that is, on the one hand, akin to the essence of technology and, on the other, fundamentally different from it. Such a realm is art."[235]

This stance is also strikingly reminiscent of Luigi Russolo's strategy proposed in his manifesto *L'Arte dei rumori* (1913), which we would propose calling a "poetic turn". Russolo and the Italian futurists in general took this stance towards the products of industrial civilisation when they refused to continue to understand the machine as

---

233 RICHARDS, John. Slippery Bows and Slow Circuits. *Musicologica Brunensia*. 2017, Vol. 52, No. 1, p. 31.

234 DUNNE, Anthony. *Hertzian Tales: Electronic Porducts, Aesthetic Experience, and Critical Design*. The MIT Press: Cambridge, Massachusetts, 2005.

235 HEIDEGGER, Martin. *The Question Concerning Technology and Other Essays*, op. cit., p. 35.

a means or a secondary production of manufacturing and looked at it as potentially an aesthetic object. The first step is an aesthetic turn, i.e. taking an aesthetic stance towards technology. The second step is a poetic turn, which grasps technology as a means of (causa efficiens) or material for (causa materialis) artistic creation.

In his text, Richards further examines historical models for a critical approach to technology, which arise from various strategies of technology's artistic understanding in the course of the 20th century. We should recall Nam June Paik and his ironic investigation of technology ("*I make technology ridiculous*")[236] riding the wave of criticism of technology in art and music, as found, for example, with Jean Tinguely and his absurd, self-destructive, pathetic, pity-inducing machines or in the music of members of the Fluxus movement (see, for example, their destructive *Piano Activities* of the 1960s). All these activities led to the creative humanisation of technology and to the application of human (non-functionalist) approaches and the ascribing of human attributes to machines. Richards also draws attention to a critical text by Frieder Nake,[237] which makes technologies secondary to their structure-forming and social consequences. Richards, working in the field of hand-crafted hardware electronics (*dirty electronics*), is developing the new critical concept of *music of things*, by which he is replacing the older *music of technology* paradigm. The basic points of his new aesthetic are the exploring of relationships between performance and composition, composing within electronics (as this strategy was formulated by David Tudor), understanding instruments as a part of a composition, and exploring the continuous transition between the musical instrument and the object.[238] Richards points out the hidden development of electroacoustic music parallel to institutional studio practice with the development of amateur electronics after the Second World War. This current of "home-made", amateur electroacoustic music (DIY) was always associated with the exploration of the audio potential of electronic components and circuits, which also entailed authentic human experience with hardware composition. We might speak of an analogy to earlier folk music that arose as a derivative of a more cultivated and better subsidised kind of music on the basis of musical instruments made by amateurs. This current of electroacoustic music forms a parallel branch of development to institutional studio practice, which fell apart definitively with the arrival of the first multimedia personal computers (Commodore Amiga 1000 etc.) in the mid-1980s. At the same time, there was physical manipulation of sound (i.e. working with electronic components) at the level of the former musical instruments. Computer music brought back the virtual practice of sound studios, *digital audio workstations* (DAW). This situation could be depicted with the following diagram:

---

236 RICHARDS, op. cit., p. 32.

237 NAKE, Frieder. There Should Be No Computer Art. *Bulletin of the Computer Art Society*, No. 18, Oct. 1971, 1–2. London, 1971.

238 RICHARDS, John. The Music of Things. *Journal of the Japanese Society for Sonic Arts*, Vol. 9, No. 2, pp. 16–20.

VIRTUAL MUSIC – SOFTWARE MEDIATED MANIPULATION OF SOUND
VS.
REAL MUSIC – MUSIC PHYSICALLY PERFORMED
ON HARDWARE "INSTRUMENTS"

There is no major difference between the two paths in terms of the possibilities they offer creative artists with respect to material and its manipulation. Software, just like hardware, offers a choice from among possibilities given in advance. The refinement and precision of the resultant form is given by the degree of the author's possibilities to influence the input conditions. In other words, the more refined the nuances and the more open the possibilities offered by the software or hardware are, the richer and more valuable the result can be. And, to the contrary, the greater the share of possibilities (whether virtual or physical) given in advance (prefabricated) is, the more limited the possibilities for creative manipulation offered by the technology will be. To put it simply using traditional terminology: for the resultant audio (musical) product, a musical instrument's value is greater to the degree that its sonic and interpretive possibilities are more open. Cakewalk is an example one might give of a relatively self-contained software, while an example of the opposite might be Pure Data's open interactive environment. An example of closed hardware might be a pedal effect, while a modular synthesizer, by contrast, is relatively open.

It would seem that the tendency towards live, individual musical performing favours physical instruments because the manipulation of physical objects is more natural for humans that manipulating sound with the use of virtual processes. Basically, we are touching upon the basic difference between thinking and acting, i.e. between intellectual and physical performance.

5.4.4 Inspiration by technologies

5.4.4.1 Leigh Landy: From electronic technologies to material

The strategy of sampling is a basic technique of remix culture, also known as plunderphonics.[239] In essence, this is an extension of Pierre Schaeffer's *musique concrète* methods. The emphasis on sampling technique helped overcome the dichotomy between sound and tone or between sound art and music. Collage and montage techniques are relevant for both fields.

In this context, we cannot fail to mention Leigh Landy, founder of the Music, Technology and Innovation – Institute for Sonic Creativity (MTI²) at De Montfort University in Leicester. His development as a theorist and composer could be summed up by the very simplified formulation: "from electroacoustic music to music based on sound". His concept of *sound-based music* consists of a shift of attention from technology to material.

239　CSERES, Jozef. Historie plundrování zvuku: Autor smrti autora je mrtev! Kdo zdědil copyright? A2, No. 27, 2007 [online]. [Accessed on 30 Jan. 2019]. Retrieved from: https://www.advojka.cz/archiv/2007/27/historie-plundrovani-zvuku.

The typology of electroacoustic music is based either on the material and method of its structuring (*musique concrète, Elektronische Musik*), the technologies used instrumentally (music for tape, computer music, synthesizer music, track music, hardware hacking, circuit bending, generative music etc.), or the method of realisation (live electronic, *musique acousmatique*, live coding etc.). There is no doubt that working with sound was the primary cause and purpose of introducing electronics in music. In the first half of the 20th century, the structing of layers of sound in time-space would have been unimaginable without new technologies such as film and magnetic tape. While some pioneers concentrated primarily on sound as a material (e.g. Pierre Schaeffer), others were carried away by technological progress in the area of new instruments and focused their attention on the application of new technologies in music and on defining the individual paradigms of music's development using technology (Karlheinz Stockhausen). It seems that a typology based on particular technologies is just as useless as talking about music history in terms of individual instruments rather than in terms of aspects of aesthetics, genre, and style.

Leigh Landy is returning to a basic, constant feature of 20th-century music: the use of sound as material for composing. He defines sound-based music as a kind of art, the basic unit of which is a sound, not a note.[240] This kind of music is not necessarily dependent upon technology, but most production uses it. One of his newer works, *Making Music with Sounds* (2012), is actually a practical textbook on working with sound relatively independently of electronic technology. It is more of a new syntax of music composed of sounds, a proposal for thinking in terms of this type of material and for possibilities for its graphic notation. And characteristically, it is intended for children in the later years of schooling who have not been marked by the history of (technological) music. Preceding this practical method was the academic treatise *Understanding the Art of Sound Organization* (2007),[241] in which the author explains his views in detail and tries to define the position of this kind of music in the framework of traditional categories like electroacoustic music, sound art etc. Landy is also the architect of the projects EARS (ElectroAcoustic Resource Site) and EARS2 with links to UNESCO, the goals of which are to popularise compositional work with sound and to make it accessible as well as to cultivate the very acts of hearing and listening.

5.4.4.2 Post-digitality in the music and aesthetics of failure

Just a few years after the beginning of the 21st century, the frequently cited text by the American composer of electronic music Kim Cascone *The Aesthetics of Failure*[242] comes to terms with the techno-optimism of the digital age. He builds upon

---

240   "[T]*he art form in which the sound, that is, not the musical note, is its basic unit.*" LANDY, Leigh. *Making Music with Sounds.* Routledge: New York, 2012.

241   LANDY, Leigh. *Understanding the Art of Sound Organization.* MIT Press: Cambridge, 2007.

242   CASCONE, Kim. The Aesthetics of Failure: 'Post-Digital' Tendencies in Contemporary Computer Music. *Computer Music Journal,* 24:4 Winter. MIT Press, 2002, pp. 12–18.

a comment made by Nicholas Negroponte, who declared at the end of the 1990s that the digital revolution had ended.[243] By this, he does not mean the end of digitality as a principle, which naturally continued to permeate all the dominant communications technologies, but rather the end of faith in its revolutionary potential. Negroponte points out that although we are surrounded and permeated by digital technologies and are living in a digital culture, the most surprising changes are taking place in other areas of our activity.

Cascone also hints at the waning of the spirit of digital optimism:

"The 'post-digital' aesthetic was developed in part as a result of the immersive experience of working in environments suffused with digital technology: computer fans whirring, laser printers churning out documents, the sonification of user-interfaces, and the muffled noise of hard drives. But more specifically, it is from the 'failure' of digital technology that this new work has emerged: glitches, bugs, application errors, system crashes, clipping, aliasing, distortion, quantization noise, and even the noise floor of computer sound cards are the raw materials composers seek to incorporate into their music."[244]

One might say that an error is often more interesting than the planned intent because it is unpredictable, complex, and the product of a technological system, and not of human thought. From a technological perspective, it is therefore authentic. In the tradition of musical thinking, only very limited work is done with errors, which are usually understood as an undesirable element in an otherwise controlled and organised order. On the other hand, we tend to understand errors as something specifically human—after all, we appreciate machines for their error-free functioning. Wherever in music history an error arises, it brings aesthetic novelty, but that is still just a departure from order, an exception that proves the rule. Possible examples are improvisation or aleatory (we should recall Cage's enchantment with technological errors, which stimulated his interest in unpredictability), as well as, perhaps, live concert performances, i.e. interpretations of a precisely notated and codified work. Is it not, in fact, the contrast between a fixed musical structure and the "imprecise" and unpredictable interpretation of the performer that is the fundamental principle of our musical culture? It does not matter whether a work is fixed in musical notation or in the form of a recording—there is still a reference form, a model with which the performer comes to terms in real time in accordance with his or her momentary judgement and current disposition.

In this context, one cannot fail to mention the proverb that one learns from one's mistakes. Firstly, an error draws attention to the weaknesses of any system, and secondly, it makes room for improvements and innovations. In addition, an error often leads to an invention or discovery, i.e. the revealing of a principle or fact that had not been previously a part of our intellectual world. For this reason, 20th-century music of this kind is called "experimental", whatever that means. After all, originality

---

243 NEGROPONTE, Nicholas. Beyond Digital. *Wired*, 6:12, 1998.

244 Ibid., pp. 12–13.

and innovation consist of the principle of bringing new elements into established ways of thinking. The medium of innovation is unimportant; what matters is the result.

The basis of the post-digital aesthetic is the error or failure, for which the word "glitch" has been coined. According to Cascone, this aesthetic began to be applied fully in the electronic dance music of the 1990s, especially in genres like house, techno, electro, drum'n'bass, drill'n'bass, trip-hop, and ambient, which he says long escaped the attention of academic debate.[245]

However, it is not just random errors that glitch is working with, but also the targeted deconstruction of data files for the purpose of creating artificial "errors" or unpredictable audio outputs. This often involves data manipulation or transmedia recoding between pictures, sounds, animations etc. In any case, it offers an unlimited field of creativity that develops the former requirements of the Italian futurists (especially Luigi Russolo) or of Pierre Schaeffer later on for new modes of listening, and especially for analytical listening.

---

245   Ibid., p. 15.

Chapter 6
Conclusions. The Influence of New Technologies on Musical Thinking

We opened our discussion of the relationship between mankind, music, and technology with Heidegger's proposed solution for the relationship between mankind and technology in the realm of the arts. Our goal has been to investigate whether and in what ways the music of the 20th and early 21st centuries has reacted to his challenge.

This book has been written because it is not just in this country that we do not yet have a satisfactorily synthesising discussion of the role of technique or technology in art music from the perspective of musical aesthetics or the philosophy of music and technology, although there are several excellent studies on specialised topics. At the heart of this book is the investigation of the impact of the technologies of the 20th and 21st centuries on the musical thinking of creators of art music.

The purpose of this book is to derive general principles inductively on the basis of historical, theoretical, and aesthetic investigation and to create categories on the basis of key words and terms that appear in the network of relationships between technologies, music, thinking, and human behaviour.

1. First we ask whether there is something like a specifically "human" music and, in opposition thereto, music that is technologically mediated. It turns out that music cannot do without technology, upon which it is directly dependent. It is not just that technologies are extensions of human perceptions, thoughts, and actions, but also that music itself is an extension of human thought. As we have discovered, certain theorists such as Collins and Young (chapter 1) directly assert that music is technology, i.e. a form of applied, instrumental thinking. Thus, we can hardly find non-technological music, some kind of Lévi-Straussian wild music of Rousseauean "noble savages" because music is a rational structure of sounding material, and every attempt to (re)produce it is necessarily bound up with the mastery of the basic principles of that structure and instrument (even if it is just the human voice). When this book discusses post-technological music, what we have in mind is not music created without the use of technology, but rather music by authors who take a critical stance towards technologically determined music (just as Postmodernism

is not necessarily the negation of Modernism, and post-internet art is not the denial of the internet's existence).

2. In relation to mankind as the creative subject with respect to the use of technology in music, we propose the identifying of four basic attitudes: techno-utopian (or techno-optimistic), techno-realistic, techno-sceptic, and post-technological. In the introduction, we propose various degrees of participation of technology in music or degrees of an author's emphasis on technology in the process of creating music, and this overlaps with two existing theories from the field of sociology: various forms of technological determinism and Bolter's and Grusin's theory of remediation. Besides giving theoretical explanations, we attempt to give examples of these basic attitudes with brief studies of the poetics of representative composers and theorists.

3. We perceive the 20th and early 21st centuries as a great arch of development in which there comes about an experimental and empirical verification of the possibilities of analogue and digital (i.e. numerical in general, not just binary) technologies for the purpose of creating music. Today, we see that electronic and digital technologies have not become the only possible form of music, as it might have seemed in the 1950s. To the contrary, the arrival of these technologies has drawn attention to a number of (anthropological) constants, which (as specific forms of social interaction) cannot be eliminated from music. It is only thanks to their temporary absence or relativisation that musical culture has become aware of their indispensability. This mainly involves the following components of the musical process:
— visuality / theatricality / performativity of music (presence of a player on stage),
— a certain degree of imperfection of performance (unpredictability),
— interactivity between the public and the player or between technology and a live player,
— the role of authorship and the completeness of a work,
— "slowness" of technological development necessary for the development of virtuosity.

As we have determined, technology has a fundamental influence on the following areas of music:

6.1 The area of musical creativity

1. **Creative intention, invention, and imagination.** Technology must not become their determinant; to the contrary, it must lead to their liberation and strengthening. Apparently the greatest threat is the loss of the meaning of musical creation because, despite frequent expectations to the contrary, that cannot be supplied to music externally by new technologies, but must be the expression of the author's internal will. Technology must be handled creatively and must become the means (causa efficiens) of realising the author's intention, invention, and imagination. While technology played a key role for invention and imagination with the interwar avant-garde, its

pragmatic function in the electroacoustic music of the latter half of the century cannot be viewed so unambiguously positively. Although technology's possibilities for sound processing contributed to the advancement of the timbral component of music, the difficulty of manipulating the technology, especially during the first decades of electroacoustic music, tended to become a barrier to free creativity. To bridge the gap, there was collaboration between composers and technicians, but these people represented two different worlds of thought or even two different cultures. That gulf was difficult to overcome and was successfully bridged mostly by composers with technical training. A peculiar approach in recent years has been technical ecology, which deliberately does without advanced technology in the creative process in favour of developing inventiveness and imagination by using simple, deliberately limited resources.

2. Historical memory and the productive function of historical amnesia. As the 20th century has shown, recording technology and storage media are becoming serious competition for the production of new music. While the music composed until the first third of the 19th century used to be put aside and forgotten (in spite of having been set down in musical notation), the arrival of audio recording brought the music of various periods into the present time and geographical location, whereby it has saturated contemporary musical culture with information. We therefore assert that while the absence of music causes the need to create new music, the oversaturation of mankind with music functions as an external factor inhibiting creativity and contributing to the loss of the meaning of musical creation. What remains is individual will and authors' need to express themselves through composed sounds. These two factors, external and internal, represent two opposite forces.

3. **New compositional strategies**. For creating new music, new strategies are being applied depending on composer's attitude towards music. Typical of technological realists is the search for subordinate, pragmatic functions for new technologies in the process of musical composition. These technologies and their processes then became an organic part of the work, without the need for them to force their logic onto the work or to draw special attention to their own existence.

As we have tried to show with several examples (chapter 5.4.2), another important factor is the adaptation of technological models in "live" music. Technologies and media bring their constructive logic into human action and thought, and this can be projected into music later, for example in the form of looping, composed additive synthesis, or remixing.

A risk factor for new creation is oversaturation with new technologies. This is the source of technological ecology and awareness of the liquidity and ephemerality of resources. Therefore, strategies are appearing for the recycling of not only existing sound material (like sampling or plunderphonics), but also audio hardware (old printed circuits, used electrical components), also involving objects made by hand by amateurs and improvisation.

4. **The emphasis on material** can take different forms in the music of the 20th and 21st centuries. Either it is the result of an effort towards making music objective (i.e. eliminating the composer's post-Romantic subjectivity, to which we drew attention in chapter 3.2), or it is a reminder that electroacoustic music was created based on the principle of manipulating sound as a material that had previously defied manipulation. The important thing from today's perspective is revising the position of electronic technology from an ontological function to a pragmatic one. Simply put, electronic technology has contributed mainly to the exploring and composing of sound. It has thereby established new paradigms of sonic art. And even if electronic technologies were hypothetically to vanish completely, they would still have left behind a change to musical thinking in the 20th and 21st centuries. Above all, electronic technologies have led to the discovery of a new timbrality or of a new methodology of working with sound material, which has enriched composed acoustic music.

6.2 The area of musical communication

1. **The breakdown and relativisation of components of music's communication model.** Individual parts of the model of linear communication transmission based on the ideas of Shannon and Weaver have been weakened, replaced, or completely eliminated. Another problem is the isolation of authors, who are trying to find a public that can understand their complicated creations. Moreover, the public for acousmatic music is newly confronted with "dead" technology that dislocates the music from the event and sound of its source, representing not only a transgression against the logic of interpretation, but also a paradox given past experience. One wonders whether the salvation and real (not utopian) future of electroacoustic music may have been the arrival of popular music that exploited electroacoustic resources while also taking the listeners into consideration. The fracturing (fragmentation, dislocation) of the spatiotemporal framework of production-reception, in which music is also produced and rehearsed as a shared experience in the "here and now", represents a major problem disrupting the established model of social communication and calling existing culture into question.

2. **The problem of instruments.** Mankind changes the surrounding world primarily through physical action. Our creative interfaces are therefore physical in nature. All older music known to us until the 20th century proceeded in this manner, using physical instruments or the human voice. New digitalised music is becoming a tool for intellectual, formal, and symbolic manipulation in virtual space. In view of the complexity of the new musical and audio structures, these manipulations are taking place in deferred time, and most of the processes remain hidden from the public. This mediated experience has an unfortunate impact not only on the public, but also on the author/performer of the music, who loses the possibility of direct communication. For this reason, new interfaces have appeared in recent years (which we can call

musical instruments in the traditional sense) for live performing, the use of which can restore direct communication between both parties.

3. **Music as the subject and object of communication.** In chapter 4.4 we tried to elaborate the problem of the relationship between music and various types of communication situations and to propose a brief typology of them. As it turns out, music is not only a subject of communication, i.e. a medium of communication (encoding emotions or the content of thought), but also an object of communication (itself being communicated and distributed in definite ways). It thereby becomes the object of sound media, distribution media, recording media, and media of reflection and meta-reflection.

6.3 The area of the musical artefact

1. **The problem of the authenticity of technological music.** A work is authentic if it is created in accordance with the author's thinking and convictions by the use of appropriate resources fulfilling the author's intentions. From a structural perspective, such a work is organic and consistent. In terms of the creative resources employed, music can be regarded as authentic if it proceeds in accordance with the possibilities and the logic of the instruments used. With technologically produced music, however, we often encounter the simulation of other (older) instruments. From this perspective, a computer simulation of a symphony orchestra is of lower value than the combination of direct digital synthesis with a probability calculation.

2. **Characteristics of the digital artefact.** In chapters 4.5 and 4.6, we explored theoretical remarks made by S. Cubitt and M. Knakkergaard. Cubitt examines the features of the digital artwork, while Knakkergaard deals with the essence of those features in the process of the shaping of digital music. Knakkergaard makes the particularly valuable observation that in view of its non-material nature, a digital work is not reproduced, but is instead always reconstructed, and that corresponds to Cubitt's of code and its resulting artefact as not being identical.

3. **Forms of the materialisation of music.** One of the most interesting findings of this book is that music can be materialised in media (materials) other than sound. Images, sculpture, and architecture are given as examples (chapter 4.8). Although some of the examples of recoding date back to the analogue era, this is a feature inherent to new media, illustrating the aforementioned principle of the non-identity of digital code and the artefact, which arises as the code's interpretation though a chosen interface. Digitality dissolves all existing media and artistic genres into the simplest possible binary code, whereupon it becomes possible to construct anything from it, whether different from or identical to the original input. In a certain sense, however, liquidity and ephemerality as basic principles of digital forms are also

applicable to creative resources and technology. The rapid succession of invention of these resources often hinders their stabilisation in music history, limiting the development of the use of their full potential. The result is a rapid succession of technologies, the possibilities of which are not sufficiently employed, making it impossible for virtuosic approaches to arise. In this sense, the tendency towards rapid innovation can be regarded as a rather negative phenomenon that harms the quality of musical culture.

6.4 The philosophical and social context of music

As the modern draws to a close, we can follow J.-F. Lyotard (chapter 5.4.1) in observing how technological development is directed by its own needs rather than the needs of artists. The subject of change is technology itself, and the need for its application is created subsequently. Here, we again encounter the problem described by P. Boulez (chapter 5.2.3), with technology preceding the needs of artistic intention, invention, and imagination (chapter 5.2.1). Technologies are an expression of modern thinking, so it is interesting to monitor their development and use in the postmodern era. We believe that during this period, what is taking place is not the elimination of technologies in society, but rather a re-evaluation of their role. While the era of Modernism swore by technology as the future of music, Postmodernism understands it as a necessary but not entirely usual part of the selection of available resources. There has been a "concealment" of technology, carrying over its principles in live, non-technological music, and creating of intuitive designs for interfaces oriented towards the user and not towards the technology itself. Technology is returning to its instrumental role and is becoming a means of realising human creativity. While in the era of Modernism, mankind was the object of the machine (instrument, tool), in the era of Postmodernism, mankind is winning back its lost dominance as the subject. In the most recent period, which is difficult for us to grasp because of the almost total lack of historical distance, one may observe the return of certain technology-oriented tendencies in the art of music. In art theory, these tendencies are usually called Neomodernism or Altermodernism (chapter 3.4).

It is very likely that the relationship between the roles of mankind and technology in the music of the 20th and 21st centuries cannot be given a definitive definition. Rather, the relationship seems to be a dynamic interaction between three worlds, in which one or another predominates on the basis of current societal, cultural, or aesthetic conditions. Our study has dealt with the formulation and analysis of these transformations.

Summary

This book examines the modalities of human relationships and technology as reflected in the musical thinking of the authors of art music of the 20th and early 21st centuries. The discursive and reference frame of the treatise consists mainly of individual artistic poetics and more general musical-aesthetic reflections embedded in the basic theoretical concepts of technology and its functions in culture and society. The departure point for the work is Heidegger's lecture *Die Frage nach Technik*, in which he suggests humanising technology through art. The following chapters examine the relationships between man, music, and technology from three points of view. Chapter 3 deals with music from a technical point of view, chapter 4 analyses the transformation of the musical artefact in the developmental arch of the 20th century from numerical abstraction through digitisation to materialisation in musical as well as non-musical art forms. Chapter 5 is a representation of man and his thinking in relation to technology in music. Here we distinguish between four basic types of attitudes in musical thinking on technology, categorised by the degree of influence attributed to technology: techno-utopian/techno-optimistic, techno-realistic, techno-sceptic, and post-technological. In the latter, we define four basic artistic strategies forming separate types: critical attitude, adaptation of technological models, recycling, and inspiration. These strategies are ranked from generally negative attitudes through specifically positive to generally positive.

Zusammenfassung

Dieses Buch untersucht die Modalitäten menschlicher Beziehungen und Technologien, die sich im musikalischen Denken von Autoren künstlicher Musik des 20. und Anfang des 21. Jahrhunderts widerspiegeln. Der diskursive Bezugsrahmen dieser Arbeit besteht hauptsächlich aus individuellen künstlerischeren Ästhetiken und allgemeinen, musikalisch-ästhetischen Reflexionen, die in grundlegende theoretische Konzepte der Technik und ihrer Funktionen in Kultur und Gesellschaft eingebettet sind. Ausgangspunkt der Arbeit ist Heideggers Vorlesung *„Die Frage nach Technik"*, in welcher der Autor die Humanisierung von Technik durch Kunst propagiert. Darüber hinaus wird der Zusammenhang zwischen Mensch, Musik und Technik untersucht. Kap. 3 befasst sich mit Musik aus technischer Sicht, Kap. 4 analysiert die Transformation des musikalischen Artefakts im Entwicklungsbogen des 20. Jahrhunderts von der numerischen Abstraktion über die Digitalisierung zur Materialisierung in musikalischen und nichtmusikalischen Kunstformen. Kap. 5 ist eine Darstellung des Menschen und seines Denkens in Bezug auf Technik in der Musik. Hier unterscheiden wir vier Grundtypen von Einstellungen des musikalischen Denkens zur Technologie, aufgegliedert nach dem Einfluss der Technologie: techno-utopisch/techno-optimistisch, techno-realistisch, technoskeptisch und posttechnologisch. In letzterer definieren wir vier grundlegende künstlerische Strategien, die unterschiedliche Typen schaffen: kritische Haltung, Adaptierung technologischer Modelle, Recycling und Inspiration. Diese Strategien werden von allgemein negativen Einstellungen über spezifisch positive bis allgemein positive Typen eingestuft.

Sommaire

La présente étude examine les modalités des relations humaines et de la technologie, qui se reflètent dans la pensée musicale des auteurs de musique sérieuse du 20ème et du début du 21ème siècle. Le cadre discursif du texte comprend principalement une poétique artistique individuelle et des réflexions musicales et esthétiques plus générales, intégrées aux concepts théoriques de la technologie et de ses fonctions dans la culture et la société. Le point de départ de l'ouvrage est l'exposé de Heidegger, Die Frage nach Technik, dans lequel l'auteur suggère d'humaniser la technique à travers l'art. De plus, la relation entre l'homme, la musique et la technologie est étudiée sous ces trois points de vue. Chap. 3 traite de la musique du point de vue technique, chap. 4 analyse la transformation de l'artefact musical dans l'arc évolutif du XXe siècle, qui va de l'abstraction numérique à la matérialisation en passant par la numérisation, sous des formes d'art musicales et non musicales. Chap. 5 est prête attention au raisonnement humain vis-à-vis de la technologie en musique. Nous distinguons ici quatre types d'attitudes de la pensée musicale à l'égard de la technologie, classées selon le degré d'influence attribué à la technologie : technoutopique/technooptimiste, technoréaliste, technosceptique et posttechnologique. Dans ce dernier cas, nous définissons quatre stratégies artistiques de base représentant quatre catégories distinctes : attitude critique, adaptation des modèles technologiques, recyclage et inspiration. Ces stratégies sont classées en fonction de leur relation à la technologie ; des attitudes généralement négatives aux attitudes spécifiquement positives et généralement positives.

References

ADORNO, Theodor W. *Philosophie der Neuen Musik*. Frankfurt a. M.: Suhrkamp Verlag, 1976.

ADORNO, Theodor W. *Schéma masové kultury* [Das Schema der Massenkultur. Kulturindustrie (Fortsetzung)]. Praha: Oikoymenh, 2009.

ARONOWITZ, S., MARTINSONS, B. and MENSER, M. (eds.). On cultural Studies. In Technoscience and Cyber Culture. NY: Routledge, 1996 cit. in Lysloff, René T. A. and Gay, Leslie C. (eds.). *Music and Technoculture. Middleton: Wesleyan University Press*, 2003.

ATTALI, Jacques. *Noise: The Political Economy of Music*. Minneapolis: University of Minnesota Press, 1985.

BARROW, John D. *The Artful Universe*. Oxford University Press, 1995.

BATTIER, Marc. A Constructivist Approach to the Analysis of Electronic Music and Audio Art – Between Instruments and Faktura. *Organised Sound* 8(3), Cambridge University Press.

BAUMAN, Zygmunt. Liquid Arts. *Theory Culture & Society*, 2007, 24.

BAUMAN, Zygmunt. *Liquid Times: Living in an Age of Uncertainty*. Cambridge: Polity Press, 2007.

BAUMAN, Zygmunt. *Úvahy o postmoderní době* [Dwa szkice o moralności ponowoczesnej; Ciało i przemoc w obliczu ponowoczesności]. Praha: Sociologické nakladatelství, 2002.

BERIO, Luciano. Prefazione. In *La musica elettronica: Testi scelti e commentati da Henri Pousseur*. Milano: Feltrinelli Editore, s. vii.

BERLAND, Jody. Postmusics. In Gerry Bloustien, Margaret Peters and Susan Luckman (eds.). *Sonic Synergies: Music, Technology, Community, Identity*. Ashgate Publishing Ltd.: Hampshire, 2008.

BJÖRK. *Compose Yourself: Entretien Björk & Karlheinz Stockhausen*. Dazed & Confused, n°23, août 1996, pp. 42–46 [online]. [Accessed: 19. 6. 2023]. Retrieved from: https://www.bjork.fr/Dazed-Confused-no23.

BOLTER, Jay David and GRUSIN, Richard Arthur. *Remediation: Understanding New Media*. Cambridge, Mass.: MIT Press, 2000.

BORN, Georgina. *Rationalizing Culture: IRCAM, Boulez and the Institutialization of the Musical Avant-Garde*. Berkeley and Los Angeles: University of California Press, 1995.

BOSSEUR, Jean-Yves. *Le sonore et le visuel – Intersections musique-arts plastiques aujourd'hui* (Les presses du réel, 1992).

BOSSIS, Bruno. The Analysis of Electroacoustic Music: From Sources to Invariants. *Organised Sound*, 2006, 11, No. 2.

BOULEZ, Pierre. Concrete (Music). In *Notes of an Apprenticeship*. A. A. Knopf, 1968.

BOULEZ, Pierre. Technology and the Composer. *Leonardo*, 1978, Vol. 11, No. 1. Retrieved from: www.jstor.org/stable/1573509.

BROCKMAN, John. *The Third Culture: Beyond the Scientific Revolution*. Simon & Schuster, 1995.

CALLON, Michael and LATOUR, Bruno. Unscrewing the Big Leviathan: How Actors Macro-Structure Reality and How Sociologists Help Them to Do So. In Karin Knorr-Cetina and Aron V. Cicourel (eds). *Advances in Social Theory and Methodology: Towards an Integration of Micro and Macro-Sociology*. Boston: Routledge, 2014.

CAMPION, Edmund. Dual Reflections: A Conversation with Kaija Saariaho and Jean-Baptiste Barriere on Music, Art, and Technology. *Computer Music Journal*. MIT Press, 2015.

CASCONE, Kim. The Aesthetics of Failure: ‚Post-Digital‘ Tendencies in Contemporary Computer Music. *Computer Music Journal*, 24:4 Winter. MIT Press, 2002.

COLLINS, Nicolas. Generative Music and Laptop Performance. *Contemporary Music Review*, 2003, Vol. 22, No. 4.

COLLINS, Nicolas. *Hardware Hacking*. Rev. 2.1, May 2004.

COLLINS, Steve and YOUNG, Sherman. *Beyond 2.0: The Future of Music*. Equinox Publishing, 2014.

Composer Steve Reich. Two Conversations with Bruce Duffie [online]. [Accessed: 9. 10. 2017]. Retrieved from: http://www.bruceduffie.com/reich.html.

CSERES, Jozef. Historie plundrování zvuku: Autor smrti autora je mrtev! Kdo zdědil copyright? A2, No. 27, 2007 [online]. [Accessed: 30. 1. 2019]. Retrieved from: https://www.advojka.cz/archiv/2007/27/historie-plundrovani-zvuku.

CSERES, Jozef. *Hudobné simulakrá*. Bratislava: Hudobné centrum, 2001.

CUBITT, Sean. Aesthetic of the Digital. In PAUL, Christiane (ed.). *A Companion to Digital Art*. Hoboken: John Wiley & Sons Inc., 2016.

DAHLHAUS, Carl. A Rejection of Material Thinking? In *Schoenberg and the New Music*. Transl. by Derrick Puffet a Alfred Clayton. Cambridge, 1987 cit. in ZAGORSKI, Marcus. *Kapitoly z estetiky seriálnej hudby*. Transl. by Robert Kolář. Edice Paralely. Bratislava: Asociácia Corpus a NM Code, 2017.

DAHLHAUS, Carl. Ästhetische Probleme der elektronischen Musik. In *Experimentelle Musik: Schriftenreihe der Akademie der Künste*. Band 7. Berlin: Gebr. Mann Verlag, 1970.

DANIELS, Dieter, NAUMANN, Sandra and THOBEN, Jan (eds.). *See This Sound: Audiovisuology Compendium. An Interdisciplinary Survey of Audiovisual Culture*. Verlag der Buchhandlung Walther König, 2010.

DANIELS, Dieter, NAUMANN, Sandra and THOBEN, Jan (eds.). *See This Sound: Audiovisuology 2. Essays*. Verlag der Buchhandlung Walther König, 2011.

DANIELS, Dieter, NAUMANN, Sandra and THOBEN, Jan (eds.). *See This Sound: Audiovisuology Reader*. Verlag der Buchhandlung Walther König, 2015.

DELALANDE, François. *Entretiens avec Xenakis: „Il faut être constamment un immigré“*. Paris: INA-Buchet/Chastel, Pierre Zech éditeur, 1997.

DELALANDE, François. *Le Son des Musiques: Entre technologie et esthétique*. Paris: INA/GRM Buchet/Chastel, 2001. Cit. in LANDY, Leigh. *Understanding the Art of Sound Organization*. Cambridge, Mass.: MIT Press, c2007.

Der blaue Reiter: Dokumente einer geistigen Bewegung. Leipzig: Verlag Philipp Reclam jun., 1986.

DLOUHÝ, Dan. *Počítačem podporovaná algoritmická kompozice* [habilitační práce]. Brno: JAMU, 2013.

DOHNALOVÁ, Lenka. *Estetické modely evropské elektroakustické hudby a elektroakustická hudba v ČR*. Praha: Univerzita Karlova, 2001.

DUNNE, Anthony. *Hertzian Tales: Electronic Porducts, Aesthetic Experience, and Critical Design*. The MIT Press: Cambridge, Massachusetts, 2005.

ECO, Umberto. *Apocalittici e integrati*. Milano: Bompiani, 1994.

Eila Hiltunen [online]. [Accessed: 5. 10. 2014]. Retrieved from: http://www.eilahiltunen.net/monument.html.

EMMERSON, Simon (ed.). *Music, Electronic Media and Culture*. Ashgate, 2000.

EMMERSON, Simon. *Living Electronic Music*. Routledge, Ashgate, 2007.

EMMERSON, Simon and LANDY, Leigh (eds.). *Expanding the Horizon of Electroacoustic Music Analysis*. Cambridge: Cambridge University Press, 2016.

EVENS, Aden. *Music, Machines and Experience: Theory out of Bounds*. Vol. 27. University of Minnesota Press, Minneapolis, 2005, Preface xi.

FARNÁ, Kateřina. Meda Mládková: *František Kupka byl vznešený a krásný člověk* [online]. [Accessed: 5. 10. 2014]. Retrieved from: http://www.novinky.cz//kultura/258654-meda-mladkova-frantisek-kupka-byl-vzneseny-a-krasny-clovek.html.

FELDMAN, Tony. *An Introduction to Digital Media*. New York: Routledge, 2003.

FLAŠAR, M., HORÁKOVÁ, J. and MACEK, P. (eds.). *Umění a nová média*. Brno: Masarykova univerzita, 2011.

FLAŠAR, Martin. Der Osten des Westens: Elektroakustische Musik in der Tschechoslowakei von 1948 bis 1992. In *Sound Exchange: experimentelle Musikkulturen in Mitteleuropa*. Saarbrücken: PFAU Verlag, 2012.

FLAŠAR, Martin. *Elektroakustická hudba* [online]. 1st edition . Brno: Masarykova univerzita, 2015. [Accessed: 29. 1. 2018]. Elportál. Retrieved from: http://is.muni.cz/elportal/?id=1308636.

FLAŠAR, Martin. Hudebním nástrojem může být dnes soustava rovnic… In VOJTĚCHOVSKÝ, Miloš. *Milan Guštar*. Praha: DOX Prague, 2013.

FLAŠAR, Martin. *Karlheinz Stockhausen: hudba a prostor*. Bachelor's thesis. Supervisor: prof. PhDr. Miloš Štědroň, CSc. Masarykova univerzita, 2003.

FLAŠAR, Martin. Minimal music jako problém figury a pozadí. In RUSINOVÁ, Zora and KRALOVIČ, Ján. *Serialita a repetícia: Zborník z Mezinárodného interdisciplinárneho sympózia*. Bratislava: Katedra teórie a dejín umenia, Vysoká škola výtvarných umení v Bratislave, 2017.

FLAŠAR, Martin. *Poème électronique, 1958: Le Corbusier, E. Varèse, I. Xenakis*. Brno: Masarykova univerzita, 2012. Spisy Masarykovy univerzit v Brně, Filozofická fakulta.

FLAŠAR, Martin. Technology or Theology? Music Beyond Technology. *Musicologica Brunensia*. Brno: Masarykova univerzita, 2017, Vol. 52, No. 1.

FLAŠAR, Martin. The Hollywood Sound Paradox: A Regress of Game Music to Film Music Origins. *Hudba – Integrácie – Interpretácie*. Nitra: Univerzita Konštantína Filozófa v Nitre, 2017, Vol. 20, No. 1.

FORRÓ, Daniel. *Domácí nahrávací studio*. Praha: Grada, 1996. Musitronika.

FORRÓ, Daniel. *MIDI: komunikac v hudbě* V Praze: Grada, 1993. Musitronika.

FORRÓ, Daniel. *Počítače a hudba*. Praha: Grada, 1994. Musitronika.

FORRÓ, Daniel. *Svět MIDI*. Praha: Grada, 1997. Musitronika.

FOUCAULT, Michel. *Of Other Spaces: Utopias and Heterotopias* [online]. [Des Espace Autres, March 1967]. In *Architecture /Mouvement/ Continuité in October*, 1984. Translated from the French by Jay Miskowiec. [Accessed: 22. 10. 2018]. Retrieved from: http://web.mit.edu/allanmc/www/foucault1.pdf.

FRIELING, Rudolf and DANIELS, Dieter (eds.). *Medien Kunst Netz 1 / Media Art Net 1: Medienkunst Im Uberblick / Survey of Media Art*. Birkhauser, 2004.

FUKAČ, Jiří. *Pojmosloví hudební komunikace*. Brno: Masarykova univerzita, 1991.

FUKAČ, Jiří. Technika a sociální funkčnost hudby. *Opus musicum*, 1972, No. 2.

FUKAČ, Jiří and MACEK, Petr. *Hudba a média: rukověť muzikologa*. Brno: Masarykova univerzita, 1998.

FUKAČ, Jiří and POLEDŇÁK, Ivan. *Úvod do hudební vědy*. Univerzita Palackého v Olomouci, 2001.

GÁL, Bernhard. Updating the History of Sound Art: Additions, Clarifications, More Questions. *Leonardo Music Journal*, 2017, 27.

GADAMER, Hans-Georg. *The Relevance of the Beautiful and Other Essays*. Cambridge University Press, 1986.

GARDNER, Howard. Igor Stravinsky: The Poetics and Politics of Music. *AVANT*, Vol. IV, No. 3, 2013.

GIBODA, Michal (ed.). *Mosty a propasti mezi vědou a uměním*. České Budějovice: Dialog vědy s uměním v nakl. Tomáš Halama, 2010.

GLENN, Martina. Orfismus [online]. Final version 9. 6. 2009. [Accessed: 4. 10. 2014]. *Artlist.cz*. Retrieved from: http://www.artmuseum.cz/smery_list.php?smer_id=87.

GORBMAN, Claudia. *Unheard Melodies: Narrative Film Music*. Indiana Univ. Press, 1987.

GRISEY, Gérard. *Gerard Grisey, an Interview* [online]. [Accessed: 10. 4. 2018]. Retrieved from: http://www.angelfire.com/music2/davidbundler/grisey.html.

GUERRA, Carlos Gustavo. The Mechanization of intelligence and the human aspects of music. In Eduardo Reck Miranda (ed.). *Readings in Music and Artificial Intelligence. Harwood academic publishers*, 2000.

GUŠTAR, Milan. *Elektrofony: historie, principy, souvislosti*. Část I, Elektromechanické nástroje. Praha: Uvnitř, 2007 a Část II, Elektronické nástroje. Praha: Uvnitř, 2008.

György Ligeti [online]. [Accessed: 5. 9. 2018]. Retrieved from: http://www.schott-music.com/shop/persons/featured/gyoergy-ligeti.

HALL, Edward T. *The Silent Language*. Doubleday & Company, Inc., Garden City, New York, 1959.

HANSLICK, Eduard. *Vom Musikalisch-Schönen: ein Beitrag zur Revision der Ästhetik der Tonkunst*, 1854. 3. verbesserte Aufl. Leipzig: Rudolph Weigel, 1865.

HARRINGTON, Richard. These Days, Kraftwerk Is Packing Light. The Washington Post. May 27, 2005. Retrieved from: https://www.washingtonpost.com/archive/lifestyle/2005/05/27/these-days-kraftwerk-is-packing-light/300d99ad-29df-4f42-8270-0cc61eafa3b7/.

HEIDEGGER, Martin. *The Question Concerning Technology and Other Essays*. Translated and with an introduction by William Lovitt. New York & London: Garland Publishing Inc., 1977.

HELFERT, Vladimír. *Česká moderní hudba. Studie o české hudební tvořivosti*. Olomouc: Index, 1936.

HELMHOLTZ, Hermann von. *Die Lehre von den Tonempfindungen als physiologische Grundlage für die Theorie der Musik*. Vieweg, 1965.

HERZFELD, Friedrich. *Musica nova*. Praha: Mladá fronta, 1966. Kolumbus.

HERZOG, Eduard. *Nové cesty hudby: sborník studií o novodobých skladebných směrech a vědeckých pohledech na hudbu*. Praha: Editio Supraphon, 1970.

HLAVÁČKOVÁ, Jitka and VOJTĚCHOVSKÝ, Miloš (eds.). *Sounds, Codes, Images*. Praha: ArtMap, 2020.

HOBSBAWM, Eric. *The Age of Extremes: A History of the World, 1914–1991*. Cit. in TAYLOR, Timothy D. *Strange Sounds: Music, Technology and Culture*. NY, London: Routledge, 2001.

HONEGGER, Arthur. *Pacific 231*. Partitura. Paris: Maurice Senart, 1924. Plate S. 6680. Retrieved from: http://petruccilibrary.ca. [Accessed: 29. 8. 2017].

HONEGGER, Arthur. *I Am a Composer*. London: Faber, 1966.

HUIZINGA, Johan. *Homo Ludens: A Study of the Play-Element in Culture*. Boston: Beacon, c1955.

CHANDLER, Daniel. Shaping and Being Shaped: Engaging With Media. *Computer-Mediated Communication Magazine* [online]. 1996. [Accessed: 13. 9. 2010]. Retrieved from: http://www.aber.ac.uk/media/Documents/short/determ.html.

CHION, Michel. *Audio-Vision: Sound on Screen*. Transl. by Claudia Gorbman. Columbia University Press, 1994.

IVERSON, Jennifer. The Emergence of Timbre: Ligeti's Synthesis of Electronic and Acoustic Music in Atmosphères. *Twentieth-Century Music*, 2010, 7.

JOHÁNEK, Filip. *Vztah technologie a rytmu v hudbě 20. a 21. století. Master's thesis*. Supervisor: PhDr. Martin Flašar, Ph.D. Brno: Masarykova univerzita, 2014.

KADUCH, Miroslav. *Česká a slovenská elektroakustická hudba 1964–1994: skladatelé, programátoři, technici, muzikologové, hudební kritici, publicisté: osobní slovník*. Ostrava: Miroslav Kaduch, 1994.

KADUCH, Miroslav. *Vývojové aspekty české a slovenské elektroakustické hudby*. Ostrava: Miroslav Kaduch, 1997.

KADUCH, Miroslav. *Záznamová technika hudby XX. století*. Ostrava: Městské kulturní středisko v Ostravě, 1982.

KANDINSKY, Wassily. *On the Spiritual in Art*. Hilla Rebay (ed.). New York: Guggenheim Foundation, 1946.

KATZ, Mark. *Capturing Sound: How Techology Has Changed Music*. Rev. ed. Berkeley: University of California Press, c2010.

KERMAN, Joseph. How We Got into Analysis, and How to Get Out. *Critical Inquiry*, Vol. 7, No. 2 (Winter, 1980) [online]. [Accessed: 29. 8. 2018]. The University of Chicago Press. Retrieved from: https://www.jstor.org/stable/1343130.

KNAKKERGAARD, Martin. Unsound Sound: On the Ontology of Sound in the Digital Age. *Leonardo Music Journal*, 2016, Vol. 26.

KONOLD, Wulf. Komponieren in der „Postmoderne". In *Hindemith Jahrbuch*, 1981, H. 10, s. 83 cit. in ZOUHAR, Vít. *Postmoderní hudba?: německá diskuse na sklonku 20. století*. Olomouc: Univerzita Palackého v Olomouci, 2004. Monografie.

KOUVARAS, Linda Ioanna. *Loading the Silence: Australian Sound Art in the Post-Digital Age*. Routledge, 2013.

KUČINSKAS, Darius and DAVISMOON, Stephen. *Music and Technologies*. Newcastle upon Tyne: Cambridge Scholars Publishing, 2013.

KUČINSKAS, Darius and KENNAWAY, Georg. *Music and Technologies 2*. Newcastle upon Tyne: Cambridge Scholars Publishing, 2014.

KUNDERA, Milan. *O hudbě a románu*. Brno: Atlantis, 2014.

LANDY, Leigh. *Making Music with Sounds*. Routledge: New York, 2012.

LANDY, Leigh. *Understanding the Art of Sound Organization*. Cambridge, Mass.: MIT Press, c2007.

LATOUR, Bruno. The Trouble with Actor-Network Theory [online]. [Accessed: 8. 10. 2015]. *Philosophia* 1997, 25. Retrieved from: http://www.ensmp.fr/~latour/popart/p67.html.

LÉBL, Vladimír and MOKRÝ, Ladislav. *Nové cesty hudby: sborník studií o novodobých skladebných směrech a vědeckých názorech na hudbu*. Praha: Státní hudební vydavatelství, 1964.

LÉBL, Vladimír. *Elektronická hudba*. Praha: Státní hudební vydavatelství, 1966.

LEVINSTON, Paul. *The Soft Edge: A Natural History and Future of the Information Revolution*. London: Routledge 1997.

LIGETI, György. Auswirkungen der elektronischen Musik. GS, Vol. 2, p. 77. Cit. in IVERSON, Jennifer. The Emergence of Timbre: Ligeti's Synthesis of Electronic and Acoustic Music in Atmosphères. *Twentieth-Century Music*, 2010, 7.

LICHT, Alan. *Sound Art: Beyond Music, between Categories*. New York: Rizzoli, 2007.

LISTER, Martin. *New Media: A Critical Introduction*. 2nd ed. Milton Park, Abingdon, Oxon: Routledge, 2009.

LYOTARD, Jean-François. *The Postmodern Explained to Children: Correspondence, 1982–1985*. Turnaround, 1992.

MANOVICH, Lev. *The Language of New Media*. Cambridge, Mass.: MIT Press, 2000.

MARCUSE, Herbert. *One-Dimensional Man. Studies in the Ideology of Advanced Industrial* Society. Boston: Beacon Press, 1966.

MAREŠ, Jakub. „Ne-sociologie“: pojetí modernosti Bruno Latoura. Diploma thesis. Supervisor: doc. PhDr. Jiří Šubrt, CSc., FF UK v Praze, 2009.

MCLUHAN, Marshall. *Understanding Media: The Extensions of Man*, GINGKO PRESS Inc., Berkeley, California, 2013.

MERRIAM, A. P. *The Anthropology of Music*. Evanston: Nothwestern University Press, 1964.

MF DNES, aho. *Češi na Expo: říše plná hudby a fantazie* [online]. 25. března 2005, 9:28. Retrieved from: http://kultura.zpravy.idnes.cz/cesi-na-expo-rise-plna-hudby-a-fantazie-dhc-/vytvarne-umeni.aspx?c=2005M071a10B.

MIRANDA, Eduardo Reck and WANDERLEY, Marcelo Mortensen. *New Digital Musical Instruments: Control And Interaction Beyond the Keyboard*. Middleton, Wisconsin: A-R Editions, 2006.

MUMFORD, Lewis. *Art and Technics*. New York: Columbia University Press, 1952.

Music 190r: Technomusicology [online]. [Accessed: 5. 9. 2016]. Retrieved from: http://wayneandwax.com/academic/Music190r-syllabus.pdf.

Music and technology. Paris: La Revue musicale, 1971.

NAKE, Frieder. There Should Be No Computer Art. *Builletin of the Computer Art Society*, No. 18, Oct. 1971, 1–2. London, 1971.

NEGROPONTE, Nicholas. Beyond Digital. *Wired*, 6:12, 1998.

ORTEGA Y GASSET, José. *Úvaha o technice a jiné eseje o vědě a filosofii* [Meditación de la técnica y otros ensayos sobre ciencia y filosofia]. Praha: Oikúmené, 2011.

OSLEJ, Dominik. *Alternatívne dotykové rozhrania v hudobnej produkcii digitálnej éry.* Master's thesis. Supervisor: Mgr. Martin Flašar, Ph.D. Brno: Masarykova univerzita, 2015.

OUELLETTE, Fernand. *Edgard Varèse.* Translated from the French by Derek Coltman. New York: The Orion Press, 1966.

PACKER, Randall and JORDAN, Ken. *Multimedia: From Wagner to Virtual Reality.* New York: W. W. Norton, c2002.

PINCH, Trevor and BIJKER, Wiebe. The Social Construction of Facts and Artifacts: Or How the Sociology of Science and the Sociology of Technology Might Benefit Each Other. In Wiebe Bijker, Thomas Hughes and Trevor Pinch (eds). *The Social Construction of Technological Systems: New Directions in the Sociology and History of Technology.* Cambridge, MA: MIT Press, 2012.

Průmysl a technika v novodobé české kultuře: [sborník sympozia pořádaného Ústavem teorie a dějin umění ČSAV ve spolupráci s Národní galerií v Praze v rámci Smetanovských dnů v Plzni ve dnech 14.-16. 3. 1985]. Praha: Ústav teorie a dějin umění Československé akademie věd, 1988.

RATAJ, Jakub and AGOSTINHO, Gilberto. *Digitální technologie v hudební tvorbě pro akustické nástroje.* Praha: AMU, 2016.

RATAJ, Michal. *Elektroakustická hudba a vybrané koncepty radioartu: problematika vymezování tvůrčích pozic v prostředí akustických umění z pohledu domácí scény radioartu.* V Praze: Kant – Karel Kerlický pro AMU, 2007. Disk, sv. 3.

RATAJ, Michal (ed.). *Zvukem do hlavy: sondy do současné audiokultury.* Praha: Akademie múzických umění v Praze, 2012.

RATAJ, Michal. O zvuku, který se hýbe v nás i kolem nás. In RATAJ, Michal et al. *Zvukoprostor - prostorozvuk.* Praha: NAMU, 2018.

REICH, Steve. Note by the Composer. In *Different Trains for String Quartet and Pre-recorded Performance Tape.* Score [online]. Hendon Music, Boosey and Hawkes, 1988. [Accessed: 31. 1. 2019]. Retrieved from: http://edoc.site.

RICHARDS, John. Slippery Bows and Slow Circuits. *Musicologica Brunensia.* 2017, Vol. 52, No. 1.

RICHARDS, John. The Music of Things. *Journal of the Japanese Society for Sonic Arts,* Vol. 9, No. 2.

ROGER, Nichols. *The Harlequin Years: Music in Paris 1917–1929.* University of California Press, 2002.

RUFER, Josef. *Das Werk Arnold Schönbergs.* Kassel, 1959.

SAARIAHO, Kaija. *Biography* [online]. [Accessed: 1. 7. 2018]. Retrieved from: http://saariaho. org/biography/.

SCRUTON, Roger. *An Intelligent Person's Guide to Modern Culture.* London: Duckworth, 1998.

SEXTON, Jamie (ed.). *Music, Sound and Multimedia: From the Live to the Virtual.* Edinburgh University Press, 2007.

SLOTERDIJK, Peter. La pensée sphérique. *BAM,* 2004, No. 2, Vies modes d'emploi. Cit. in BOURRIAUD, Nicolas. Altermodern. In *Altermodern: Tate Triennial 2009.* London: Tate Publishing, 2009.

SLOTERDIJK, Peter. *Regeln für den Menschenpark. Ein Antwortschreiben zu Heideggers Brief über den Humanismus.* Sonderdruck. Edition Suhrkamp: Frankfurt am Main, 1999.

SMOLKA, Martin. *Remix, Redream, Reflight* (2000) [online]. [Accessed: 5. 3. 2018]. Retrieved from: http://www.martinsmolka.com/works/remix.html.

SNOW, Charles Percy. *The two cultures*. Cambridge: Cambridge University Press, 1998.

SOURIAU, Étienne. *Encyklopedie estetiky*. Praha: Victoria Publishing, 1994.

STRAVINSKIJ, Igor and CRAFT, Robert. *Dialogues and A Diary*. Doubleday & Company, 1963.

STRAVINSKY, Igor. *Poetics of Music in the Form of Six Lextures*. Translated by Arthur Knodel and Ingolf Dahl. Cambridge: Harvard University Press, 1947.

ŠMAJS, Josef and KROB, Josef. *Úvod do ontologie* [online]. [Accessed: 15. 7. 2017]. Retrieved from: https://www.phil.muni.cz/fil/eo/skripta/kapitola_1.html. 2nd edition corrected and expanded. Brno: Masarykova univerzita Brno, 1994.

TAYLOR, Timothy D. *Strange Sounds: Music, Technology and Culture*. NY, London: Routledge, 2001.

The BBVA Foundation recognizes Finnish composer Kaija Saariaho for breaking down the divisions between acoustic and electronic music [online]. [Accessed: 2. 7. 2018]. Retrieved from: www.bbva.com.

TIFFON, Vincent. *Musique mixte : Repères historiques. Un diaporama avec la définition et les principaux repères historiques de la musique mixte, sur ariam-idf.com* [online]. [Accessed: 2. 7. 2018]. 18. 10. 2012, rev. 28. 8. 2017. Retrieved from: http://www.ariam-idf.com/sites/default/files/18-support-tiffon.pdf.

TICHÝ, Vladimír. Chaos a hudba. In *Živá hudba XIV: sborník prací Hudební fakulty Akademie múzických umění*. Praha: Státní pedagogické nakladatelství, 2005.

TONDL, Ladislav. *Věda, technika a společnost: Soudobé tendence a transformace vzájemných vazeb*. Praha: FILOSOFIA, 1994.

TROJAN, Jan. Mechanicko-muzikální umělecké figuríny aneb O neuvěřitelných zážitcích ve staré brněnské Redutě. *Opus musicum*, 2005, 4.

Varèse and Contemporary Music, Trend, May-June, 1934, pp. 124–128. Cit. in OUELLETTE, Fernand. *A Biography of Edgard Varèse*. Translated from the French by Derek Coltman. New York: Orion Press, 1968.

VARÈSE, Edgard. *Die Befreiung des Klangs*. Übersetzt von R. Riehn. In CHARBONNIER, Georges. *Entretiens avec Edgard Varèse*. Paris: Belfond, 1970.

VARÈSE, Edgard. Que la musique sonne. *391*, No. 5, June 1917, New York, s. 2. Cit. in OUELLETTE, F. *A Biography of Edgard Varèse*. Translated from the French by Derek Coltman. New York: Orion Press, 1968.

Velký sociologický slovník. II, P-Ž. Praha: Karolinum, 1996.

VERMEULEN, Timotheus and AKKER, Robin van den. Notes on Metamodernism. *Journal of Aesthetics & Culture*, 2: 1, 5677, 2010.

VOJTĚCH, Ivan. Technika a hudební senzibilita. In *Průmysl a technika v novodobé české kultuře: [sborník sympozia pořádaného Ústavem teorie a dějin umění ČSAV ve spolupráci s Národní galerií v Praze v rámci Smetanovských dnů v Plzni ve dnech 14.-16. 3. 1985]*. Praha: Ústav teorie a dějin umění Československé akademie věd, 1988.

Výroční zpráva Centra základního výzkumu AMU a MU [online]. [Accessed: 10. 7. 2017]. Retrieved from: https://www.amu.cz/cs/ovvp/msmt/programy-podpory-vav/centra-zakladniho-vyzkumu/dokumentace/vyrocni-zprava-centra-zakladniho-vyzkumu-amu-mu-za-rok-2005.

VYSLOUŽIL, Jiří and FUKAČ, Jiří. *Slovník české hudební kultury*. Praha: Editio Supraphon, 1997.

WINNER, Langdon. *Autonomous Technology: Technics out of Control as a Theme in Political Thought*. Cambridge, MA: MIT Press, 1977, pp. 192–210.

XENAKIS, Iannis. *Formalized Music: Thought and Mathematics in Composition*. Additional material compiled and edited by Sharon Kanach. Stuyvesant, N.Y.: Pendragon Press, 1992.

ZAGORSKI, Marcus. *Kapitoly z estetiky seriálnej hudby*. Transl. by Robert Kolář. Edice Paralely. Bratislava: Asociácia Corpus a NM Code, 2017.

ZOUHAR, Vít. *Postmoderní hudba?: německá diskuse na sklonku 20. století*. Olomouc: Univerzita Palackého v Olomouci, 2004. Monografie.

Index of Names

Index of Compositions

Index of Terms

MASARYK
UNIVERSITY
MONOGRAPHS
VOL. 3

Martin FLAŠAR

Mankind – Music – Technology

Technology in the Musical Thinking of the 20th and Early 21st Centuries

Published as the 3rd volume in the series „Masaryk University Monographs"
supported by Scientia est Potentia Fund.

Translated by Mark Newkirk
Cover photo by Archive of Petr Nikl
Edited by Alena Mizerová
Layout and typesetting by Pavel Křepela
Printed by Powerprint
Published by Masaryk University Press, Žerotínovo nám. 617/9, 601 77 Brno, CZ
First edition

ISBN 978-80-280-0364-7
ISBN 978-80-280-0365-4 (online ; pdf)

https://doi.org/10.5817/CZ.MUNI.M280-0365-2024